P9-CMF-603

GIFT OF
ANNI. II. ET PHILLIS
1920

RAMBLES IN COLONIAL BYWAYS

WILLIAM LINCOLN HUDSON.

OLD CHURCH AT ECONOMY, PENNSYLVANIA

OLD CHURCH AT ECONOMY, PENNSYLVANIA

Rambles in Colonial Byways

BY

RUFUS ROCKWELL WILSON

Illustrated from drawings
By William Lincoln Hudson
and from photographs

Vol. II.

Philadelphia & London
J. B. Lippincott Company
1901

12396

Copyright, 1900
By J. B. Lippincott Company

Electrotyped and Printed by
J. B. Lippincott Company, Philadelphia, U. S. A.

Contents

CHAPTER		PAGE
VIII.	ALONG THE EASTERN SHORE . . .	9
IX.	THE CITY OF THE FRIENDS . . .	42
X.	PENN'S MANOR AND BEYOND . . .	75
XI.	GOD'S PECULIAR PEOPLE . . .	107
XII.	BETHLEHEM AND AROUND THERE . .	139
XIII.	THREE GROUPS OF GERMAN MYSTICS .	173
XIV.	THROUGH WASHINGTON'S COUNTRY . .	206
XV.	YORKTOWN AND HER NEIGHBORS . .	239

Illustrations

PAGE

OLD CHURCH, ECONOMY, PENNSYLVANIA *Frontispiece*

MOUNT CUSTIS, AN EASTERN SHORE HOMESTEAD .   18

OLD SWEDES' CHURCH, PHILADELPHIA   .   .   44

OLD ST. DAVID'S, RADNOR, PENNSYLVANIA .   .   86

SAAL AND SARON, EPHRATA, PENNSYLVANIA   .   122

SISTERS' HOUSE, BETHLEHEM, PENNSYLVANIA   .   144

MOUNT VERNON, HOME OF WASHINGTON .   .   222

RUINED TOWER OF JAMESTOWN CHURCH   .   .   252

RAMBLES IN COLONIAL BYWAYS

❧❧

CHAPTER VIII

ALONG THE EASTERN SHORE

IT was a wise friend who counselled us
to begin our tour of the Eastern Shore at
Eastville. By the Eastern Shore is meant
the peninsula bounded on the north and east
by Delaware Bay, on the south and east by
the Atlantic, and on the west by the Chesapeake, a quaint and venerable region containing about one-third of Maryland and
two counties of Virginia. Bountifully endowed by nature, it is also, for the man
who loves the past, a land of delight. When
New York was yet a wilderness and Plymouth a virgin forest, men of English birth
were growing tobacco, dredging oysters, and
shooting wild fowl on the Eastern Shore.
The descendants of these first settlers still
follow the same pursuits. Moreover, locked
away for the better part of three hundred

years in this neglected nook, they cling with affectionate tenacity to the manners and customs, the traditions and modes of life, of their forefathers, so that one finds on the peninsula the indolent old-time existence and the broad hospitality of an earlier age, along with the careless air of ancient gentility, tempered and made piquant by an aristocratic exclusiveness.

And sleepy Eastville, near its southern end, is the Eastern Shore in miniature. Only during the last dozen years has it had easy connection with the outer world, and even now it feels but dubiously the intestine stir of modern ideas. Rows of white, low-roofed houses line its single dusty street, with two or three country stores and a couple of roomy taverns dropped in between, while a court-house and clerk's office bear witness to the fact that it is the shire town of the ancient county of Northampton. Eastville is the centre of a land overflowing with milk and honey, and above it and below it are the homes of people who in the golden days before the Civil War counted their slaves by hundreds and their acres by thousands,—old families whose ancestors date far back into the seventeenth century as men of importance and power.

Beside the inlets and rivers that deeply indent the shores of the peninsula stand the roomy dwellings of these old families out-looking over the bay, with lawns in front smooth as green velvet, dipping down to the water's edge. Such is the old Parker man-sion, standing at the junction of two creeks, a fine old house surrounded by a thick clus-ter of trees, with large porches front and back, paved with marble slabs, and a long colonnade running from the kitchen to the main building. In these old dwellings the kitchen is almost always separated from the house, connected with it only by this cov-ered way, thus securing coolness to the house, at the same time providing shelter from the rain for the dainty dishes, delicate yet simple, such as only the negro cook of the South can compound. Erstwhile the cook held absolute sway in her quarters, with a parcel of jolly, grinning little negro boys as pages. The mistress might rule the household and the master the fields, but in her own dominions, portly Dinah, with white teeth showing beneath her red turban, reigned supreme.

The name of Parker is repeated on every page of the early history of the lower Eastern Shore; and so is that of the well-known Custis family, high in social position and pride of birth, one of the later descendants of which was the first husband of Martha Washington. Arlington, the whilom seat of the Custises, faces the Chesapeake a dozen miles below Eastville, and is reached by a drive along a grass-grown road that never carries one out of sight of the placid waters of the bay. No vestige of the mansion remains; but near its former site are a couple of crumbling and weather-beaten tombstones that once stood, as is customary throughout Virginia, close to the old homestead. The inscription on the most elaborate of the two tells the visitor that beneath it lies the body of John Custis, who died " aged seventy-one years and yet lived but seven years which was the space of time he kept a bachelor's house at Arlington on the Eastern shore of Virginia." On another side of the tomb

12

is the statement, duly chiselled in the marble, that "the foregoing inscription was placed on this stone by the direction of the deceased." The father-in-law of Mrs. Washington, if not an unhappy husband, was surely one of the most eccentric of men.

John Custis's tomb and its companion grave are the only visible reminders of the glory of Arlington, but it is an easy and pleasant task to recreate the vanished era in which it had its place. A hard-swearing, hard-drinking, hard-driving,—ay, and a hard-working lot, when the humor was on them,—were these men of the Eastern Shore, of a period when "the planter who had the most hoes at work was the best man,"—to every hoe a slave or a convict; when tobacco stood for all that was notable and characteristic in life and manners; when every large proprietor was in direct communication with England; when the ships of Bristol and London brought supplies directly to the planter's own wharf, and his eldest son, as well as his tobacco, was often shipped across in return.

The wives, sisters, and sweethearts of

these dead and gone worthies were their comrades and competitors in the saddle or the dugout. Though they delighted to gossip of Chinese silks, brocades, lutestring, taffeta, sarsenet, ginghams, and camlets,— not forgetting pyramids and turbans, jewelled stomachers, breast-knots, and high-heeled shoes for the minuet,—they were also at home on the bridle-path and comfortable on the pillion; they rode to hounds, and were clever in the handling of a tiller or the trimming of a sail. Irving describes them as going to balls on their side-saddles, with the scarlet riding-habit drawn over the white satin gown. "In the flashing canoe, ticklish and fascinating, they maintained," we are told, "the equilibrium of their bodies and their tempers with an expertness that was not ungraceful, and with a graciousness in which long training had made them expert. The dugout, dancing in the creek, waited upon their freaks and caprices with uses as frequent and familiar as those which pertained to the wagon or the gig,—to race in a ladies' regatta, or to run out to the old-country ship in the offing, with its pulse-stirring news of fashions and revolutions, battles and brocades, cloaks, cardinals, and convicts, sultana plumes, French falls, and the fate of nations."

The spirit of the age was knightly, and the sword, not the purse, the symbol of distinction. When the Revolution came, the Maryland section of the Eastern Shore was warmly attached to the patriot cause; but in the Virginia counties of Northampton and Accomac the Loyalists were numerous; and one of the earlier episodes of the seven years' struggle was a small civil war on the peninsula. Dunmore, expelled from the mainland of Virginia, took refuge in Accomac, and soon had some hundreds of Tories under arms. The situation looked grave; but Matthew Ward Tilghman, chairman of the Maryland Committee of Safety, and his seven Eastern Shore colleagues proved equal to it. They promptly called out two companies of militia and suppressed the rising before the worst came of it. Afterwards the two victorious companies, with a third from the Eastern Shore, were embodied in Smallwood's regiment, the famous First of the

Maryland line. Perhaps the most brilliant exploit of the Revolution was the stand made by four hundred of this regiment, under Lord Stirling, on the fatal day of Long Island. In six successive charges they beat back the greatly superior pursuing force of Cornwallis, and were on the point of dislodging him entirely when Grant, with nine fresh regiments, overwhelmed them by a rear attack.

The Second Maryland Regiment was wholly recruited on the Eastern Shore, while Pulaski's legion and Baylor's cavalry, besides several other organizations, also drew largely from the peninsula. It sent, moreover, seven hundred militiamen, under Gist, to the battles of Brandywine and Germantown; furnished Washington with one of his most valued staff officers, Lieutenant-Colonel Tench Tilghman, and at the same time gave to the councils of the State and nation Cæsar Rodney, Matthew Ward, and his kinsman Edward Tilghman, William Paca, Thomas Ringgold, and other men of high character and unusual ability.

Though the War of 1812 revived the old

military traditions, the golden age of the Eastern Shore went out with the Revolution. Slipshod and sluttish husbandry, that counted it cheaper to take up new land than to foster and restore the old, bore speedy fruit in mortgaged crops and acres, while the gradual substitution of wheat and corn for tobacco marked the increasing poverty of a soil worn out in its youth, and which sank from good to bad and from bad to worse. So things went on till sixty years ago. Since then they have changed for the better, and, though checked for a time by the loss of slaves and the turmoil of civil war, the upward movement is still in progress. Fertilizers have been introduced and improved breeds of stock. Machinery has taken the place of hand-labor in farm-work; and worthless fields have been limed and drained into fertility.

In other respects, however, the Eastern Shore remains unchanged,—a severed fragment of colonial America. The new-comer from over the seas has gone on to the cheaper and freer lands of the West, and the busy Northern man, as he hurries by, barely pauses to knock at its doors. And so the years, as they wax and wane, find the same population on the same soil,—a population composed, now as of old, of three classes,— the " gentleman born," the " plain people," and the negroes. Each class, save in exceptional cases, marries strictly within its own limits; and half a dozen surnames will frequently include nearly the whole gentry of a county, the appellations of present-day bride and bridegroom tallying exactly with those on the century-old tombstones of their common ancestors. Again, for the upper classes there is still but one church, the Anglican. They have listened in the same seats to the same service for generations, and, more often than not, they take the communion service from a chalice that was new in the days of the Restoration. Some of them can show ancestral souvenirs of the Martyr King. Easter and Whitsuntide remain universally recognized holidays, and antique observances still cluster around the minor festivals. Thus, freedom from change has made the Eastern Shore a land of serenity and dignity; but its confines are too nar-

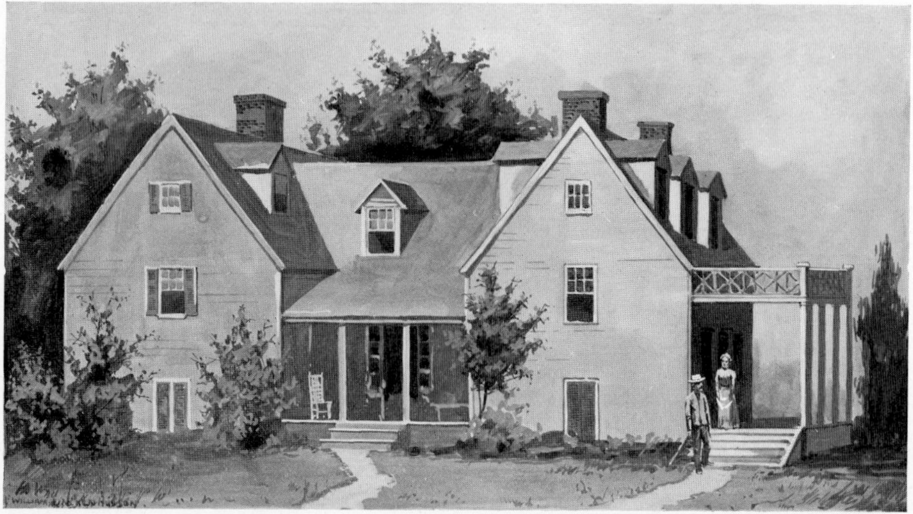

MOUNT CUSTIS, AN EASTERN SHORE HOMESTEAD.

row for youthful enterprises. It has no imperial possibilities, and must ever be a nook.

Proof of many of these things was before us as we drove to and from Arlington, and a little later set out from Eastville for a further exploration of the Eastern Shore. Our destination was the island of Chincoteague, on the Atlantic side of the peninsula, and the road led through the hamlet of Anancock and the sound of the same name, the latter a loop or skein of salt coves widening up between green mounds and golden bluffs, and terminating at an exquisite landing, where several creeks pour into the cove from the estates of well-to-do planters. Drummondtown, the county-seat of Accomac, was also passed on the way. Three miles beyond we halted for a half-hour's rest at Mount Custis, a roomy, rambling old house standing close to the shores of a creek, which, as its name indicates, once belonged to the masters of Arlington, and in the late afternoon found ourselves on board the tiny steamer "Widgeon" with Chincoteague in the eastern offing.

Outlying along the Atlantic coast and extending southward for more than fifty miles from the mouth of Delaware Bay is a narrow strip of sandy beach, its western side washed by the waters of a landlocked sound and its eastern beat upon by the surges of the ocean. Its southern end, called Assateague, is separated from the mainland by Chincoteague Sound, and lying within this sound is the island of the same name, only its southern extremity being thrust out from its snug hiding-place behind Assateague and exposed to the Atlantic. Yet at every turn the visitor to Chincoteague, with its gray-green waters and its far horizons, feels the majesty and pervasive presence of the sea. The air has a salty, pungent quality; all along the shore lie craft of one sort or another, and every grown man carries in his face the mellow marks of sun and wind, for the people of Chincoteague get their living from the sea, which affords them, directly or indirectly, not only food and drink, but clothing and shelter. Nobody asks alms, and want and theft are unknown. At the island's feet lie oyster-beds of wondrous richness, and any skilled worker can

earn a living wage during nine months of
the year. Winter, however, is the season
of greatest activity, and then Chincoteague's
fleet of oyster-boats is busy from sunrise to
sunset. Early morning finds the oystermen
hoisting sail; all day long they can be seen
on the western horizon groping for the hid-
den treasure; and when twilight falls, scores
of their little craft, beating homeward, make
the harbor, facing the mainland, a snow-
storm of canvas.

Truth is that Chincoteague is merely a
standing-place and lodging-house for its inhabitants. The visitor discovers, to his surprise and delight, that it is also the breed-
ing-place of a race of ponies unlike any other
in the world. Some are watched and tended
on private lands, but most of them, to the
number of half a thousand, inhabit the common pastures at the south end of the island,
whence, when the weather is bad and the
waves high, scores of the little fellows are
sometimes swept away and lost. Skirting
the coast in a boat, one sees them feeding
together on the pastures or standing knee-
deep in the salt water, the breeze scattering

their tangled manes. They are about thirteen hands high, nearly all sorrels or bays, and are fine-bodied and neatly limbed. The yearlings, which are never gelded, come through the winter with shaggy coats that are in rags and shreds before the summer is old, and still show tattered remnants at the yearly penning and branding in August. No one knows whence they came or how long they have inhabited the island, but as they have the head and eyes of the Arabian, the supposition is that the ancestors of the present generation came ashore from a wreck in colony times.

When we left Chincoteague and its contented fisherfolk it was to journey, by way of Berlin and Snow Hill, to Crisfield on the hither side of the peninsula. That intrepid sailor, Stephen Decatur, was born near Berlin, and Snow Hill has a peaceful history dating back to the seventeenth century, while Crisfield, facing the beautiful waters of Tangier Sound, has been aptly described as a town of oysters reared on oyster-shells. A man on building bent buys a lot at the bottom of the harbor, encloses it with piles, and then purchases enough oyster-shells to raise it above high-water mark. The product of this singular practice is a village which stands, as it were, up to its knees in the water of a little harbor that cuts jaw-like into the end of a small peninsula thickly flecked with the homes of fishermen and oystermen. Moreover, the railroad that runs through the length of the town, terminating at the water's edge, rests on a road-bed of oyster-shells as firm and solid as broken granite. Along the harbor front, and all built upon shells, are the huge, barn-like packing-houses in which centres the chief interest of Crisfield,—the shucking and packing of oysters for the Northern market. These come mainly from the beds of Tangier Sound, perhaps the finest in the world; dredging for them gives constant employment to a fleet of several hundred sloops and schooners, and the annual returns from the trade mount into the millions. In winter thousands of bushels of oysters are sent off from Crisfield simply shelled, drained, and pressed into kegs or cans; but later in the season they are canned in hermetically sealed tins, in which condition they will keep for years.

Crisfield and its oyster trade belong to the present. Tangier Island, across the Sound, is part and parcel of the past. Much homely matter anent this sequestered nook is to be found in "The Parson of the Islands," a book dealing with the life story of a humble fisherman evangelist who labored with such effect in an unpromising field that to this day, when a flag is raised on the little island chapels, signifying "Preacher amongst us from the mainland," the waters fill with canoes scudding down from every point of the compass. The island parson kept a canoe, called "The Methodist," to haul the preachers to and fro, and in the second war with England, when the whole British army established a permanent camp on Tangier Island, and thence ravaged the shores of the Chesapeake, burnt Washington, and sought to capture Baltimore, this unpretending gospeller preached to them, and prevailed upon them to respect the immemorial camp-meeting groves.

Tangier, like Chincoteague, is a land of

far horizons, of restless gray-green water, of vivid marsh grass, and of sweet salt air. Like Chincoteague, it is the home of a hardy, primitive people, who fear God and find no fault with their lot. The benevolent bay yields a living to all who are able and willing to work, and it is the boast of the islanders that there are neither drunkards, paupers, nor criminals among them. Less could be said of a more favored community.

From Crisfield a railroad—its route a giant interrogation point—runs by way of Westover, the centre of the berry culture of the Eastern Shore, to Cambridge on the Choptank. This stream is the noblest water-course of the peninsula,—at its mouth, a superb sound, curtained with islands, several miles wide; farther inland a net-work of coves and deep creeks, to whose beachy margins slope the lawns and orchards of many fine old homesteads; and Cambridge is a gem worthy of so exquisite a setting. A salt creek, bordered with snug old mansions of wood and brick, creeps up behind the tree-embowered town; and a clear spring rises under an open dome in the village square, which faces an ivy-covered court-house, while a little way removed from the business centre stands an old Episcopal church, garbed in living green and sur-rounded with mouldering gravestones carved with crests, shields, and ciphers.

There are a score of other objects in Cambridge to please an artist's eye, and another quaint and beautiful hamlet is Oxford, on the northern shore of the Choptank, where Robert Morris, the financier of the Revolution, passed the greater part of his boyhood. Threadhaven Creek—a perfect fiord, unexcelled by any low-lying Danish or Swedish marine landscapes—enters the Choptank at Oxford, and a few miles away, at the head of the same stream, nestles the quiet town of Easton. The road from Oxford to Easton leads past Whitemarsh Church, a dilapidated but picturesque structure dating back to the seventeenth century, and in an oak-shaded dell about a quarter of a mile from the latter place stands another house of worship which was already old when the republic was born. This is a Quaker meeting-house of antique design, which, according to tradition, once

numbered William Penn among its worshippers. His followers still meet within
its walls on First and Fifth Days.

Easton suggests in more ways than one
the stately affectations of a bygone time;
and nearby St. Michael's, at the mouth of
Miles River, though now the chief depot of
the oyster trade of the Middle Chesapeake,
boasts intimate association with the great
men and stirring events of the Revolutionary period. The ship-builders of St. Michael's have plied their craft for two hundred
and fifty years, and when the eighteenth century was still young, vessels launched from
their yards controlled the coastwise commerce from New England to the West Indies. The country bottoms of the Chesapeake traded with Liverpool and Bristol;
smuggled for Holland and France, and when
the Revolution came, turned to privateering
and became as hornets and wasps in the face
of the foe. The records show that in less
than six years two hundred and forty-eight
vessels sailed out of the bay—"and this with
a British fleet at Hampton Roads and inside
the capes all the time"—to fight and capture

ships and small craft at the very gates of
the enemy's ports, in the British and Irish
Channels, off the North Cape, on the coasts
of Spain and Portugal, in the East and West
Indies, and in the Pacific Ocean. This
record was repeated in 1812, when at least
one Chesapeake privateer, the "Chasseur,"
made a true viking's record. Armed with
twelve guns, manned by men from the Eastern Shore, and commanded by Captain
Thomas Boyle, she captured eighty vessels,
thirty-two of equal force and eighteen her
superior in guns and men. Boyle was born
at Marblehead in 1776, married in Baltimore
in 1794, and died at sea in 1825. He commanded a ship at sixteen, was a husband
two years later, and made a dramatic end
of a romantic and glorious career at forty-
nine.

From either Easton or St. Michael's it is
an easy and inviting detour to Wye House
and Wye Island,—two storied shrines of the
Eastern Shore. Called after the little river
which rises in the Cambrian Hills, and
mingling its waters with those of the Severn,
flows out through Bristol Channel to the At-

lantic, there are few American water-ways
more lovely than the Wye. Its banks are
free from the sombre borders of marsh which
fringes most of its sister streams, and its
channel, from head to mouth, sweeps between bold bluffs of woodland and smiling
fields, dotted by the manor-houses of men
and women whose ancestors dispensed stately
hospitalities in these same homes more than
a century ago. And nowhere, in those days
of pleasantness and peace, had the stranger
more generous welcome than was sure
to be given him by the master of Wye
House.

This sturdy domicile, built of bricks
brought over from England, was burned in
1781, when a British marauding party looted
the plantation and the mansion; but near
its site stands another spacious structure,
which invites the present-day wayfarer in
the name of all the generations of gentle,
kindly folk who have dwelt there since Edward Lloyd, in 1668, set up his son Philemon to be lord of the manor of Wye and
master of Wye House. The main building
of two lofty stories is connected by corridors

with one-storied wings, presenting a façade of two hundred feet, looking out upon a noble, tree-strewn lawn, and over engirdling woods to Wye River and the island beyond. Behind the mansion is a flower-garden, and in the rear of that the family burial-ground, where is gathered the dust of many worthies and dames of the blood of the Lloyds. Here beneath a battered shield supported by mortuary emblems sleeps that Henrietta Maria Lloyd who had the hapless wife of Charles I. for her godmother; and here, without a stone or a stake to mark the spot, rests all that was mortal of William Paca, thrice member of Congress, twice governor of Maryland, and signer of the Declaration of Independence.

Moving memories also color the later history of Wye House, whose present gracious mistress is the granddaughter of Colonel John Eager Howard of Revolutionary fame and of Francis Scott Key, author of "The Star-Spangled Banner." Eighty-odd years ago the steward or bailiff of the Lloyd estate was a certain Captain Anthony, of St. Michael's. This man was the owner of a negro boy who escaped from bondage, and became before middle age the foremost figure of his race. In 1881, Frederick Douglass, white-haired and honored of men, was moved to revisit the scenes of his childhood and his thrall, and one day found himself at the door of Wye House. The son of its master gave him welcome, and when he had made known the motive of his visit, he was conducted over the estate. Each spot he remembered and described with all its childish associations,—here a spring, there a hedge, a lane, a field, a tree,—and the whole heart of the man seemed to go out to the place as he passed from ghost to ghost as in a dream.

Then befell a strange thing. Standing mute and musing for a while, he said softly and low, as one who communes with himself, "Over in them woods was whar me and Marse Dan uster trap rabbits." Marse Dan was the son of the whilom master of Wye House and Douglass's playmate in childhood. Thus, humor blending with pathos, was the ennobling lesson of an unusual life compacted into the homely reflection and phrase of a barefoot slave boy. Afterwards Douglass plucked flowers from the graves of the dead Lloyds he had known, and at the table drank to the health of the master of the old house and his children, "that they and their descendants may worthily maintain the character and the fame of their ancestors."

Philemon Lloyd, first master of Wye House, at his death left to his only daughter thousands of fertile acres on the Wye. This daughter, by her marriage to Samuel Chew, a planter of ancient lineage and great wealth, who early left her a widow, added to her already large possessions; and one of her bequests to her son Philemon, when her time came to die, was the island of three thousand acres which faces both Wye House and the mouth of the Wye, and which he passed on to his two sisters.

Mary Chew became the wife of William Paca, and Margaret was wooed and won by John Beale Bordley, the descendant of an old Yorkshire family, the last of the admiralty judges of Maryland under the provincial government, and an earnest supporter of the

patriot cause in the Revolution. No trace
remains of the many-roomed house at the
lower end of Wye Island, built by Samuel
Chew of material brought from England,
and long occupied by Judge Bordley and his
family; but the mansion which Paca's son
erected is still standing at the island's upper
end, and promises to outlast another century. The Paca homestead crowns a commanding eminence, whence it looks down
upon the narrows separating it from Wye
House, and controls a view of long reaches
of rich acres once the inheritance of the
Lloyds and Chews, and still owned, to a
great extent, by their descendants. The land
naturally slopes downward from the river-
bluff, but has been terraced up until it forms
a broad plateau, sufficient to accommodate
not only the house, but the garden which
surrounded it, and which, with its extensive
conservatories, was once a gayer paradise of
shrubs and flowers.

Wye Hall, though fallen from its former
state, gives ample evidence of its early grandeur. The building is in the Doric style,
the central portion square, with spacious,

lofty columned porticoes, and stretching
away on either side are covered arcades,
terminating, the one in the kitchen and
offices, the other in the grand parlor or
ball-room. This grand parlor is a beautiful
and stately room, the high ceiling orna-
mented with handsome stucco-work and the
walls hung with family portraits by the
fathers of our native art. Among them is
a full-length picture of Governor Paca.
Painted by the elder Peale, and in his best
manner, it shows a man of commanding
presence and strikingly handsome features.
The rich dress and easy carriage betoken
high birth and breeding, the dark eye and
well-chiselled mouth character and firmness.

The entrance-hall and corridors of Wye
House are, likewise, noble apartments, and
here, also, one wanders in the past. The
Signer's solid and substantial bookcase, on
the shelves of which yet stand the volumes
of his law library, and the tables where he
played short whist with his Revolutionary
associates are still used by his descendants.
Here, too, are the antique chairs which
graced the executive mansion at Annapolis

when Paca was governor, and which were loaned for use when Washington resigned his commission. The career of William Paca has been briefly sketched in another place. His last days were spent in delightful retirement on Wye Island, than which there can be imagined no more charming retreat for a man of wealth and culture wearied with the burdens of public life in trying times, and there he died in October, 1799. During his last illness " he conversed with perfect resignation on his approaching dissolution, and cheerfully submitted to sickness and death under a deep conviction of the unerring wisdom and goodness of his heavenly Father, and of the redemption of the world by our Lord and Saviour, Jesus Christ. To the faith and charity of a Christian he added the civil virtues of a gentleman,—fond as a husband, indulgent as a father, constant as a friend, and kind as a master." Such is the testimony of some appreciative friend, whose manuscript, without date or name to lead to the identification of its author, is preserved among the family archives at Wye Hall.

When we left Wye Island it was to board

one of the steamboats trading to Baltimore, which weekly visit the bays and creeks of the Eastern Shore, and which carried us, during the early hours of a sunny afternoon, down the Wye and west across Eastern Bay to the lower end of Kent Island, where was established the first colony of white men on the Maryland shores of the Chesapeake. Kent Island belies its name, for it is, in fact, a peninsula connected with the mainland by a short and narrow isthmus, and in shape very like the hammer of an old-fashioned musket; and it has no ruins and no town; yet at every stage of the northward drive, past pleasant farms and fishing beaches to the mouth of the Chester, one is made to feel that he is riding over historic ground.

About a year after the landing at Plymouth Rock William Claiborne established a trading post at the southern end of Kent Island. This Claiborne, a man of enterprise and daring, was secretary to Sir John Harvey, then governor of Virginia. Obtaining a grant from Harvey, he claimed Kent Island and the bay for the colony of Virginia, and when the Calverts founded the Catholic settlement of St. Mary's, he disputed their jurisdiction over the Eastern Shore, and carried the question through the colonial and English courts. Defeated at every point, Claiborne resolutely maintained his ground, and when Sir Leonard Calvert came with an armed force, met him in the bay and completely routed him off Kent Point in what was probably the first naval battle fought in American waters. Then, taking the offensive in his turn, Claiborne marched into Western Maryland and swept Calvert across the Potomac into Virginia. In the seesaw of factions neither could long keep uppermost, for in 1646 Lord Baltimore's authority was reëstablished on the Western Shore, the Eastern submitting to him at the end of another year.

Still, Claiborne's defeat was not final, for in 1653 he returned from England with a commission from the Puritan government then in power to reduce the royalist provinces about the Chesapeake. Lord Baltimore's rule was overturned, Kent Island restored to Claiborne, and a government selected by him established on the Western Shore. It retained control until Charles II., on his accession, reinstated the Calverts, with full power over the whole colony. Then Claiborne, deeming the contest hopeless, withdrew to Virginia. There he founded the county of New Kent, in memory of the isle he had struggled for half a lifetime to retain; represented his new home in the colonial Legislature, and ended by a gallant death at the Indian battle of Moncock a career that reads like a romance in even the barest statement.

In one respect, however, Claiborne's influence still abides on the Eastern Shore. When he first colonized Kent Island he brought with him from Jamestown the Rev. Richard James, a clergyman of the Church of England, who became the founder of the first Christian church on the soil of Maryland. This episode of Claiborne's Virginia chaplain gave the Anglican Church a permanent foothold on the Eastern Shore, for as the colony of the Isle of Kent spread gradually to the mainland, wherever it fixed itself the parish was organized, the church was built, and the magistrate's duties devolved upon the vestrymen and churchwardens. All traces of the structure in which James officiated have been long since lost, but more than one of the ancient churches that issued therefrom lie within the reach of a drive from Kent, by way of Queenstown and Centreville, to Chestertown, near the head of the beautiful river from which it takes its name.

The first churches built upon the mainland of the Eastern Shore were those of Chester and Wye. The ruins of the former, which was of extraordinary size, may still be seen near Centreville, while the latter, more gently dealt with by the years and the elements, occupies its original site on the Wye, its black-glazed bricks continually telling the story of its age to the worshippers who yet gather within its walls. Both churches were built between the years 1640 and 1650. Most of the old parish churches of the Eastern Shore, however, were erected between 1693 and 1700. The oldest of these later edifices which preserves its original shape and construction is that of St. Luke's, which tops a low hill, a few miles south of Chestertown, a square edifice, with apsidal chancel, heavy galleries, and spireless roof. The vestry-room is a detached building, with brick floor and huge fireplace at either end, suggestive of the dignified, ease-loving lords of the manor, who of old time administered the discipline of church and state.

Our zigzag tour of the Eastern Shore ended at Chestertown, an old place with a decayed college overlooking it, a loamy country round, and a broad and placid river laving its feet, but not before we had made visits to The Hermitage, a historic homestead facing one of the loveliest reaches of the Chester, which from the year 1660 to that of 1881 never passed out of the hands of a Richard Tilghman, and to the old church of St. Paul's, in the county of Kent. This noble relic of bygone days flanks the ancient thoroughfare which was, in Revolutionary days, the main line of travel between Annapolis and Philadelphia, and has counted seven generations among its worshippers.

A bold and curving stream sweeps close up under the shadows of the giant oaks which shade the church, and which must have been sturdy trees when it was built in

1693. The church itself is of the type before described, and around it lies a quiet God's Acre, kept bright with flowers and fresh with verdure by loving hands. The ground is sacred with forgotten graves, and the sexton's spade, when hollowing a bed for some new sleeper, seldom fails to turn out relics of the unknown dead. In such a church-yard might Gray have wandered as he framed the stanzas of his " Elegy," and sight of this lovely resting-place, where, as the sun sweeps around his daily course, the shadows of the old church falls successively on every sodded bed, remains one of the lasting mellow memories of ten days of delightful strolling along the Eastern Shore.

CHAPTER IX

TIME and change have touched Philadelphia with gentle hand. The Friends are, in the great essentials, still its dominant class, and this fact appears not only in its asylums, its hospitals, and its practical methods of helping men to help themselves, but in a prudence of thought and action that is ever reluctant to prefer the new to the old. Thus it is that no New World city harbors more numerous or more eloquent reminders of the past, or in ancient buildings and landmarks bound up with great names and great events offers to the wayfarer a richer or more varied store of historic associations.

Not to the coming of Penn, but to the issue of a dream cherished by Gustavus Adolphus, attaches the oldest authentic legend of Philadelphia. A score of years before the Quaker leader was born the heroic and generous Swede, moved thereto by the bigotry and poverty of the age in which he lived, conceived the idea of founding in America a city "where every man should have enough to eat and toleration to worship God as he chose." Gustavus's life ended before his dream could be fulfilled, but eleven years later the girl Queen Christina and her chancellor despatched an expedition in the dead king's name. This colony of "New Sweden," as it was called, effected a lodging-place along the banks of the Schuylkill and Delaware, in that part of Philadelphia now known as Southwark.

The narrow strip of ground on which the Swedes made their homes is given over in these latter days to ship stores, junk-shops, and salty, tarry smells, while a long line of ships, come and to go, walls in the view of the river; but if one might be frisked by the mere magic of a wish back to the middle years of the seventeenth century, he would find instead the low huts of the Norseland pioneers dotting green banks on the edge of a gloomy, unbroken forest, with hemlocks and nut trees nodding atop. Here dwelt, in peace and plenty, and "great idleness," if an old chronicle is to be believed, the long forgotten Swansons, Keens, Bensons, Kocks, and Rambos, some of them mighty hunters when the deer came close up to the little settlement and nightly could be heard the cry of panthers or bark of wolves. At Passajungh was the humble white-nut dwelling of Commander Sven Schute, whom Christina called her " brave and fearless lieutenant," and at " Manajungh on the Skorkihl" there was a stout fort of logs filled in with sand and stones.

Descendants on the female side of these first settlers are still to be found in the city, but Philadelphia's only relic in stone and mortar of the men who were once lords of all the land on which it was built is Gloria Dei, better known as Old Swedes' Church. Each successive sovereign of Sweden, loyal to the favorite idea of Gustavus, kept affectionate watch over the tiny settlement on the Delaware, and when the colonists begged " that godly men might be sent to them to instruct their children, and help themselves to lead lives well pleasing to God," two clergymen, Rudman and Bjork, were de-

OLD SWEDES' CHURCH, PHILADELPHIA.

spatched by Charles XII. in answer to their
prayer. These missionaries reached the colony in June, 1697, and were received, as
the ancient record states, "with astonishment and tears of joy." Soon after their
arrival Gloria Dei was built in a fervor of
pious zeal, carpenters and masons giving
their work, and the good pastor daily carrying the hod. When it was finished Swedes,
Quakers, and Indians came to wonder at its
grandeur, and it long remained the most important structure in the little hamlet.

Old Swedes' holds its original site in
Southwark, banked in by the sunken graves
of its early worshippers. The main body of
the building is unaltered to the present day.
The carvings inside, the bell, and the communion service were sent out from the
motherland, given by the king " to his faithful subjects in the far western wilderness;"
and from Sweden came also the chubby gilt
cherubs in the choir which still sustain the
open Bible, with the speaking inscription,
" The people who sat in darkness have seen
a great light." Tablets in the chancel record
the sacrifices and sufferings of the early

pastors of the church who sleep within its walls. The last of these was Nicholas Collin, whose period of zealous service covered the better part of fifty years, and who with his devoted wife Hannah is buried just below the little altar. Another familiar face in Gloria Dei in the opening years of the century was that of Collin's friend, Alexander Wilson, then the half-starved, ill-paid master of a little school at nearby Kingsessing. The great ornithologist is buried in the graveyard of the church in which he asked that he should be laid to rest, as it was "a silent, shady place, where the birds would be apt to come and sing over his grave."

When Old Swedes' was built the only house nearby was that of Swan Swanson, from whose three sons Penn, when he came, bought the land to lay out his town of Philadelphia. That was in 1682. A small band of pioneers had preceded the Proprietor, and he was followed by three-and-twenty ships, filled with Quakers of all classes. The city, speedily laid out by Thomas Holme, extended from river to river, and appeared magnificent—on paper;

but, truth to tell, most of the new-comers following the example of the Swedes, who gave them kindly welcome, built their homes in the corner by the Delaware; and for nearly a hundred years the town consisted of but three or four streets, running parallel with that stream. Back of these streets lay a gloomy forest, drained by creeks, which cut the town into three or four parts before emptying into the Delaware. As late as the opening year of the Revolution Philadelphia extended only from Christian to Callowhill Streets, north and south, and until well on in the present century Frankford, Roxborough, and Germantown were reckoned distant hamlets, being seldom visited by the people of the town.

On a " pleasant hill" overlooking the river, and with a noble sweep of forest land between, the Proprietor reserved a lot for himself, on which he had built the house, which he gave to his daughter Lætitia. The brick and other material for this house were brought from England, and within its walls Penn passed most of the busy and fruitful days of his first visit, preferring it to the costly and imposing pile he had reared at Pennsbury. The searcher after the site of the Lætitia House finds it in Lætitia Court, between Chestnut and Market, Second and Front Streets,—a narrow, dirty alley, cut off from the sunlight by the backs of the great importing houses which now cover the wooded glades where, in the Proprietor's time, deer ranged at will. Elsewhere in Philadelphia there are few traces of the reign of the Penns. One of the few is what is known as Lansdowne, now included in Fairmount Park, which was once owned and occupied by John Penn, governor of the colony in its last days of submission to the British crown.

The Lætitia House was the first brick building erected in Philadelphia. Most of the dwellings built during the earlier years of the Quaker occupancy, some of which are still standing within the precincts of the "old town," were of black and red English brick, or of mortar mixed with broken stone and mica. They were, as a rule, small, hipped-roofed, two-storied structures, infe-rior in every way to those now occupied by people of moderate incomes. Gradually, however, as time went on, the more shrewd or fortunate among the Quakers acquired large means, while the steady growth of the town attracted to it a number of men, not followers of Penn, who brought with them or soon became possessed of much solid wealth. From these changed conditions resulted a division into two classes of the social life of the town, and the building of many splendid houses, the grandeur of which is reflected in more than one diary and chronicle of the period. Among these were the Wharton House, in Southwark; Wilton, the estate of Joseph Turner, in the Neck; Woodlands, Governor Hamilton's great house at Blockley Hill; the Carpenter mansion, which stood at Seventh and Chestnut Streets, surrounded by magnificent grounds; the spacious home of Isaac Norris on Third Street; the Pemberton country-seat, on the present site of the Naval Asylum; and, chief of all, Stenton, on the city-ward site of Germantown.

Stenton, "a palace in its day," according to old Watson, was built in 1731 by James

Logan, a keen-witted Scotchman turned
Quaker, who, as agent of the Proprietor,
stood between Penn and his debts on one
hand and an impatient, grasping colonial
Assembly on the other, serving both with
fidelity and to good purpose. He was generous as well as shrewd, and at his death
left the residue of a large estate to the public,
including the splendid bequest of the Logan-
ian Library, a literary treasure-house at any
time, but invaluable a century and a half
ago, when books were luxuries only for the
wealthy. Logan was also the trusted friend
of the Indians, who came in large deputa-
tions to visit him, and pitched their wig-
wams on the great lawn at Stenton. Logan,
the famous Mingo chief, was the namesake
of the good Quaker, and, in youth, was often
numbered among the latter's savage guests.

Stenton, in its builder's time, was the seat
of a sober but large hospitality, and the centre of the social life of the Quakers. Here
gathered the grave, mild-mannered men and
the quiet, sweet-faced women, who look down
upon us from old family portraits, and whose
rare and admirable traits included a perfect

simplicity and that repose which can belong only to people who have never doubted their own social position. "The men and women who met at Stenton," writes one of Logan's descendants, "talked no scandal and spoke not of money." Logan's home was the resort of the colonial governors, not only of Pennsylvania but other of the provinces; and among his frequent guests were William Allen, Isaac Norris, the three Pembertons, and that Nicholas Waln who, educated for the bar, after long practice in the courts, so took to heart the moral short-comings of his fellow-lawyers that he fell into a dangerous illness. He rose from his bed a changed man, went into the meeting and became a weighty and powerful preacher.

However, not all of the guests at Stenton were as serious-minded as Waln. The men could laugh and jest on occasion; and their wives and daughters were pretty sure to display a woman's love of finery, setting off their beauty by white satin petticoats, worked in flowers, pearl satin gowns, gold chains, and seals engraven with their arms. Nor are lacking stray hints of love and courtship which lend a winsome interest to the old house, for pretty Hannah Logan's lover, returning with her from a summer day's fishing in the Wissahickon, writes in his diary that when they "came home there was so large a company for tea, that Hannah and I were set at a side table, and there we supped—on nectar and ambrosia." Another of Stenton's daughters was Deborah Logan, a fair and gracious woman in youth and old age, who in the "Penn and Logan Correspondence," compiled by her and by her given to the world, has given us a faithful and winning picture of the age in which she lived, an age marked by a lack of self-assertion and an inborn hatred of brag, whose influence abides in the Philadelphia of to-day.

Different in religion, tastes, and habits from the Friends were the men of wealth and their families who constituted a not inconsiderable portion of Philadelphia's polite society during its first century of existence. These were the merchants and ship-owners, who, though not followers of Penn, had been attracted to his town by its successful growth, and who, opening a trade to the West Indies and England, from small ventures quickly amassed colossal fortunes. The wives and daughters of these merchant princes, most of whom could show ancestral bearings, followed afar off the reports of English fashions. They rode on horseback or went in sedan-chairs to pay visits; their kitchens swarmed with slaves and white redemptionists; they dined and danced, and —gambled; and they worshipped of a Sunday in a church dedicated to the Anglican creed.

The parish of Christ Church was thirty-two years old when the present building was commenced in 1727. William of Orange was an active promoter of the parish, and the service of plate now in use in the church was a gift from Anne. Designed by the architect of Independence Hall, Christ Church presents many points of similarity to that historic structure, and is likewise closely identified with the struggle for independence. Here worshipped General and Lady Washington, Samuel and John Adams, Patrick Henry, James Madison, John Hancock, and Richard Henry Lee. Under its roof the Episcopal Church in America was organized, in 1785, and within its walls is now housed a rare and interesting collection of ancient volumes, furniture, pictures, and tablets, each of interest to the student and lover of the past.

One of the first rectors of Christ Church was a Rev. Mr. Coombe. He was a Loyalist, and during the early days of the Revolution returned to England, where he finally became chaplain to George III. It is probably from him or one of his family that an alley, a short distance above Christ Church, and running eastward, takes its name. Here it was that the namesake and heir of William Penn, when he came over to play the prince in the colony, once got into a brawl. He was spending an evening in Enoch Story's inn, when he fell to quarrelling with some of his fellow-citizens who were acting as the watch. The sober Friends, who had little patience with princely debauchees, arrested the young fellow for this affray, whereupon he incontinently forsook the Society for the Church of England, in which faith the descendants of Penn have ever since remained.

Coombe's Alley, in the younger Penn's time, was a prosperous quarter, and it still bears traces of better days. In 1795 it had a very large population for such narrow limits,—boasting its half-dozen boarding-houses, its merchants and laborers, its soldiers and mariners, its bakers and hucksters. Nor was it without its cares and troubles; for during the famous epidemic of 1793 thirty-two people died in the course of a year in this one small street. The old houses still standing in it are built of the red and black bricks so plentiful in the city's youth. In most cases curious wooden projections, like unfinished roofs, divide the first story from the second, making the latter look as though they had been an after-thought.

The chimes of Christ Church, which on July 4, 1776, proclaimed the tidings of independence, were paid for by the proceeds of a lottery conducted by Benjamin Franklin. The printer-patriot takes his rest under a flat marble slab in the crowded burial-ground at the corner of Fifth and Arch Streets, but

his life and works are still vital influences in
the city of his adoption. In truth, his ad-
vent into the town at the age of seventeen
marks the date of the birth of the intellectual
life of Philadelphia. Blending shrewd common sense with keen, fine humor, and a ca-
pacity for winning and holding friends, the
young printer, in a space of time signally
brief, gained recognition as a leader in the
town. Its old respectabilities eyed him
askance, but following where he led, made
him clerk of Assembly, postmaster, and agent
to England, or looked on with grudging as-
sent as, out of the unlikely material of his
fellow-workmen, he established his Junto,
or philosophic club, and founded the first sub-
scription library in the country, the first fire
and military companies in the colony, and
the first academy in the town, just as, in
after-years, they held aloof while he, with
two or three other Philadelphia radicals,
united with Southerners and New Eng-
landers in signing the papers which gave freedom to the country and immortality to its
makers.

Though every effort for the improvement

of colonial Philadelphia can be traced to
Franklin, one comes closest to him, perhaps,
in the old library which grew out of his
Junto club, and which, guarded by an effigy
of its founder, long stood close beside the
State-House, just out of Chestnut Street,
but has now been removed to Park Avenue
and Locust Street. Inside are dusky recesses filled with dusty time-worn folios, and
from one of the galleries the great Minerva
which presided over the deliberations of
the Continental Congress looks down upon
a desk and clock once owned and used by
William Penn. The noise and hurry of the
modern world never reach this cloistered
recess, crowded with the shades of scholars
dead generations ago, and an hour spent
therein is a page from the past that will
linger long in the memory.

A quaint hipped-roofed house standing on
Front Street, a few doors above Dock, recalls another significant incident in the life
of Franklin. To this house, erstwhile occupied by one generation after another of
Quakers, he was conducted upon his return
from England, just before the opening of

the Revolution. Philadelphia had for some time presented the spectacle of an exceptionally temperate and prudent community slowly rousing to temperate, prudent resistance to injustice. The Friends, prompted by motives for which we can scarcely blame them, were opposed to armed rebellion; so were the great merchants, to whom a war with England threatened financial ruin. Facing the other way were a numerous body of citizens eager for the moment of conflict. Loyalist and patriot alike waited anxiously for Franklin and his first words of counsel. The Friends in a body met him as he landed, and without a word, in solemn procession, escorted him to the Front Street house. Entering, they all seated themselves, still silent, waiting for the Spirit of God first to speak through some of them, when, as we are told, Franklin stood up and cried out with power, "To arms, my friends, to arms!" That his warning fell on reluctant if unheeding ears is known to all. The sudden influx of the leaders of the Revolution, in the stormy days that followed, pushed the Quaker class and the

Tory families for the moment to the wall; and during the most glorious period of the city's history her old rulers, with few exceptions, yielded their places to strangers.

Still another reminder of the Philadelphia that Franklin knew is the house of his long-time friend, John Bartram, which yet stands near the Schuylkill, on the Gray's Ferry Road. The former home of the Quaker botanist is of graystone, hewn from the solid rock and put in place in 1734 by Bartram's own hands; for among his other accomplishments he reckoned that of practical stonemason. A dense mat of ivy, out of which peep two windows, cover its northern end. The south end, nearly free from vines, is also pierced with two large windows, the sills thereof curiously carved in stone-work. Between these two windows, upper and lower, a smooth, square block of stone has been carved with this inscription:

'Tis God alone, Almighty Lord,
The Holy One by me adored.
John Bartram, 1770.

Dormer-windows jut out from the roof of the old house, and between its two projecting wings runs a wooden porch, supported by a massive stone pillar, the front covered by an aged but still lusty Virginia creeper. Time has worked small change in the ancient structure. The great fireplace in its central room has been filled up, and the old Franklin stove, a present, mayhap, from Benjamin himself, has been removed from the sitting-room, but beyond this everything stands as it did in its first owner's time. Back of the sitting-room, in the wing looking towards the south, is an airy apartment that once did duty as a conservatory. Beside this room is the botanist's study, with windows facing the south and east. It was here in later years that Alexander Wilson wrote the opening pages of his great work on ornithology, under the patronage and aided by the suggestions of William Bartram, the successor of his father John, and himself a naturalist of learning and repute.

Against the front of the house grows a Jerusalem " Christ's-thorn," and on one side of it a gnarled and tangled yew-tree, both planted by the elder Bartram's hands. Thence the famous botanic garden, the first one on this continent, which the good Quaker constructed untaught, planting it with trees and shrubs gathered by himself in countless journeys through the wilderness, slopes gently downward to the banks of the Schuylkill. When Charles Kingsley visited Philadelphia, some years ago, his first request was to be taken to this old garden, which has now become a grove of trees, rare and various, of native and foreign growth,— deciduous trees and evergreens of many varieties, blossoming shrubs, white and red cedars, spruce, pines, and firs, thick with shade and spicy with odor. At the garden's lower edge and close to the river once stood a cider-mill, of which all that remains is a great embedded rock, hewn flat, with a circular groove in it, in which a stone dragged by horses revolved, crushing the apples to pulp. A channel cut through the rock leading from the groove served to convey the juice from the mill. It was a piece of Bartram's own handiwork, another example of the combining of the practical and ideal in his sturdy nature. Not far from this old cider-mill stands a stone marking the grave of one of Bartram's servants, an aged black, one time a slave, for even the Quakers held slaves in colony times. At the time of the old negro's death, however, he was a freeman, and had been for years, for Bartram was one of the earliest emancipators of slaves in America.

All that Bartram, whom Linnæus pronounced "the greatest of living botanists," was enabled to achieve he owed, in the main, to his own efforts. His life was of the simplest character; and to the last he retained the habits and customs of the plain farmer folk, of whom he accounted himself one. Touching also in its modesty and simplicity is his own account of how he became a botanist. "One day," he wrote in his later years, "I was busy in holding my plough, and being aweary I sat me beneath the shade of a tree to rest myself. I cast mine eyes upon a daisy. I plucked the pretty flower, and viewing it with more closeness than common farmers are wont to bestow upon a weed, I observed therein many curious and distinct parts, each perfect in itself, and each in its way tending to enhance the beauty of the flower. 'What a shame,' said something within my mind, 'that thou hast spent so many years in the ruthless destroying of that which the Lord in His infinite goodness hath made so perfect in its humble place without thy trying to understand one of the simplest leaves!' This thought awakened my curiosity, for these are not the thoughts to which I had been accustomed. I returned to my plough once more; but this new desire for inquiry into the perfections the Lord hath granted to all about us did not quit my mind; nor hath it since."

The path upon which he thus set forth made the Quaker farmer the peer and fellow of the greatest naturalists of his time, and in his later days royal botanist for the provinces. Bartram lived to the age of eighty, hale and strong to the last, his only trouble being his dread that the ravages of the Revolution might reach his peaceful garden. His fear was groundless, for all alike reverenced and loved the gentle old man. His death occurred on the morrow of the battle of Brandywine.

Philadelphia, in 1774, had grown to be a

thriving, well-conditioned, prosperous city of thirty thousand inhabitants, the largest in the colonies, and, thanks to the genius of Franklin, paved, lighted, and ordered in a way almost unknown in any other town of that period. It was, also, as nearly as possible, the central point of the colonies. Thus both its position and its condition drew to it the strangers from the North and the South, who began to appear in the streets and public places in the late summer of 1774. Few of these strangers were commonplace; most of them gave evidence of distinction, and all were prompt in setting about the work that had brought them from their widely-scattered homes.

The members of the first colonial Congress having found, on reaching Philadelphia, that the State-House was already occupied by the Provincial Assembly, determined to hold their meetings in the hall, on Chestnut Street above Third, built by the Honorable Society of Carpenters, and still used by them. Accordingly, on the morning of September 5 they assembled at the City Tavern, where most of them were quartered, and went thence together to this little hall. We are told that the Quakers watched the little procession gloomily, but it was made up of men who have assumed for us heroic proportions. There were John and Samuel Adams, of Massachusetts, the latter with stern, set face of the Puritan type; the venerable Stephen Hopkins, of Rhode Island; Roger Sherman, of Connecticut, tall and grave; John Jay, of New York, with birth and breeding written in his clean-cut features; Thomas McKean, of Pennsylvania, an Anak among patriots, and lank Cæsar Rodney, of Delaware. There, too, were Christopher Gadsden and the two Rutledges, from South Carolina, while Peyton Randolph, full of years and honors, headed a delegation from Virginia which included Patrick Henry, Richard Henry Lee, and another better known than any of them, with his soldier's fame won on hard-fought fields,—George Washington, of Mount Vernon. What the grave, silent Virginia colonel had done was known to every onlooker. What he was yet to do no one dreamed, but we may easily believe that the people who lined the streets that sunny September morning felt dumbly what Henry said for those who met him in the Congress, "Washington is unquestionably the greatest of them all."

The work done in the assembly-room of the hall of the Carpenters in the autumn days of 1774 cleared the way for the call to arms. When the Congress met again, in May of the following year, it held its deliberations in the State-House, and thenceforward the history of the country takes this long, old-fashioned structure of red brick, with its white marble facings and thick window-sashes, as its central point of interest. In the little square before it gathered excited groups of patriots and Loyalists on the memorable days and still more memorable nights when within its walls, behind closed doors, the delegates of thirteen colonies were debating a resolution to declare them independent. On July 2, 1776, the resolution was passed. "A greater question," says Adams, "perhaps never was decided among men."

The Declaration was signed by John Hancock and Charles Thomson, president and secretary of the Congress, on the Fourth of July, this act taking place in the east room of the State-House on the lower floor, where during the next four weeks the other members of the Congress also affixed their signatures. The Declaration had been written by Thomas Jefferson in his lodging-house, which stood until recently at the south-west corner of Market and Seventh Streets. It was made public on the morrow of the Fourth, but was not officially given to the people until noonday on the 8th of July, when it was read to a great crowd in the State-House yard. The stage on which the reader stood was a rough platform, built some years before by David Rittenhouse, the astronomer, as an observatory from which to note certain important movements of the planets.

The use to which its builder had put it had resulted in the first determination of the dimensions of the solar system; and now serving a not less noble purpose, it heralded a platform of human rights broad enough for the whole world to stand upon. Cheers

rent the welkin when the reading of the
Declaration was finished; bonfires were
lighted; the chimes of Christ Church rang
until nightfall, and the old bell in the State-
House tower gave a new and noisy meaning
to the words inscribed on its side a quarter
of a century before,—"Proclaim liberty
throughout the land and to all the inhabitants
thereof."

Thus the Republic was born. The story
of the days of storm and stress that followed has been written again and again, and
ever finds new chroniclers; but over one
act of the great Congress that adopted the
Declaration the pen must always linger with
affectionate touch. On June 14, 1777, it
was resolved by the Congress "that the flag
of the United States be thirteen stripes alternately red and white, and that the union
be thirteen white stars, in a blue field, rep-
resenting a new constellation." The first
flag was modelled under the personal supervision of Washington, who was then in Philadelphia, and a committee from the Congress. They called upon Mrs. Elizabeth
Ross, who conducted an upholstery shop in

the little house yet standing at 239 Arch Street; and from a rough draft which Washington had made she prepared the first flag. The general's design contained stars of six points, but Mrs. Ross thought that five points would make them more symmetrical. She completed the flag in twenty-four hours, and at Fort Schuyler, New York, a few weeks later, it received its baptism of fire. "Betsy" Ross was appointed by Congress to be the manufacturer of the government flags, and she followed this occupation for many years, being succeeded by her children.

In September, 1777, the British entered Philadelphia, and it was not reoccupied by the patriot army till 1779. Meantime in its northern suburbs was fought the desperate and luckless battle of Germantown. About many of the old houses of that village hang pulse-moving legends of the one eventful day in its history. Chief among these is the Chew House, built in 1763, about which the fight raged furiously for hours. This house was held by Colonel Musgrave and six companies so long that a gallant lad, the

Chevalier de Manduit, with Colonel Laurens, crept up to fire it with a wisp of straw. They escaped under a shower of balls, while a young man who had followed them fell dead at the first shot.

Another old house at the corner of Main Street and West Walnut Lane was used as a hospital and amputating-room, while the Wistar House, built in 1744, was occupied by some of the British officers, one of whom was General Agnew, "a cheerful and heartsome young man," according to tradition. As he passed out to join his command he encountered the old servant Justinia at work in the garden, and bade her hide in the cellar until the fighting was at an end. But Justinia refused to obey, and had not finished hoeing her cabbages when Agnew was carried in wounded unto death, a decoration which he wore on his breast having offered a mark for a patriot rifleman. A quaint room of the Wistar House, now filled with relics of early times, is the one in which the heartsome young officer breathed out his life. His blood still stains the floor.

Yet another reminder of the Revolution

is to be encountered in a stroll about Germantown, for in the yard of St. Michael's Lutheran Church sleeps one who played a useful if humble part in the struggle. Chris. Ludwick was a Dutch baker of Germantown, who had saved a comfortable fortune before the commencement of the seven years' war. Half of this property he offered to the service of his country, swearing at the same time never to shave until her freedom was accomplished. Washington gave him charge of the ovens of the army, and Baker-General Ludwick, with his great grizzled beard and big voice, was a familiar and not unheroic figure in the camp. He died an old man of eighty, in 1801, leaving his entire fortune for the education of the poor.

After the Revolution came the making of the Constitution and the setting afoot of the Union, with Philadelphia as the national capital. The city's condition during the years in which it was controlled by Washington's simple high-bred court is known to every reader of history. In the great house once occupied by Richard Penn, afterwards owned by Robert Morris, and gone long since from the south side of Market Street, Washington had his home from 1791 to 1797. It was deemed the fittest dwelling in the city for the President of the new nation, and must have well deserved to be called a mansion. There are many pleasing pictures of the life led there by Washington and his family, but none half so winsome and delightful as that of a girl friend of Nelly Custis, who spent a night in the President's house. " When ten o'clock came," she tells us, " Mrs. Washington retired, and her granddaughter accompanied her, and read a chapter and psalm from the old family Bible. All then knelt together in prayer, and when Mrs. Washington's maid had prepared her for bed Nelly sang a soothing hymn, and, leaning over her, received from her some words of counsel and her kiss and blessing."

One other picture, and the last, of the Philadelphia of a century ago. The time was March 4, 1797, and a vast crowd had assembled in the State-House to witness the inauguration of John Adams as Washington's successor. Few in the throng, however,

gave heed to the entrance of the new chief
executive. Instead, every eye was bent upon
Washington, for the people knew it was to
be the last public appearance of their idol.
"He wore," writes an eye-witness, "a full
suit of black velvet, his hair powdered and
in a bag, diamond knee-buckles, and a light
sword with gray scabbard." Beside him
was the new Vice-President, Jefferson, awk-
ward and ungainly; and nearby was the
boyish Madison and the burly Knox. When
Adams had read his inaugural and left the
room the crowd cheered, but did not move.
Jefferson, after some courteous parley, took
precedence of Washington, and went out.
Still the people remained motionless, watching the noble figure in black; nor did any
one stir until Washington descended from
the platform and left the hall to follow and
pay his respects to the new President. Then
they and all the crowd in the streets moved
after him, but in silence. Upon the thresh-
old of the President's lodgings he turned and
faced this multitude of nameless friends.
"No man ever saw him so moved." The tears
rolled unchecked down his cheeks. Then

he bowed slowly and low and went within. After he had gone a smothered sound, not unlike a sob, went up from the crowd, for they knew that their hero had passed away to be seen of them no more.

CHAPTER X

PENN'S MANOR AND BEYOND

ONE of a dozen delightful outings lying in the way of the sojourner in Philadelphia or its suburbs takes one to the ancient borough of Bristol. Set down on the western bank of the Delaware, midway between Trenton and Philadelphia, Bristol has seen more than two centuries sweep by since the beginning of its settlement, and all about the town there are traces remaining of the birth years of the republic, and even of colonial times, in narrow and irregular streets, and olden houses with chimneys at the gable ends, and in family heirlooms treasured in these antique dwellings by descendants of the first settlers. A large part of Bristol is built of brick, giving the town a substantial and comfortable appearance; Mill Street, the main thoroughfare, has many old business houses on it, and Radcliffe Street, stretching through its vista of shade-trees, for a long distance along the river's bank, is lined with fine mansions, most of them set in spacious grounds, and all commanding views of the Delaware, creeping seaward between grassy and wooded banks.

Peace and rest dwell the twelvemonth through in Bristol, and it is fitting that they do, for the town is the eastern gateway to the Penn's Wood of other days, and six miles to the north of it, up the Delaware, is Pennsbury Manor, the spot where stood the mansion erected and occupied by William Penn. The estate originally consisted of above six thousand acres, bounded by Welcome Creek and Governor's Creek. A tract of three hundred acres, including the site of the homestead, is now owned as a farm by William Penn Crozer. Many years ago a visitor to the place noted the fact that nine gnarled cherry-trees were then standing as the remains of Penn's cherry hedge along the lane. One poor stump is all that is now left, and this relic is fast crumbling into dust, but the well that belonged to the old mansion still gives its pure water to the thirsty or curious wayfarer.

The manor-house was of brick, and might possibly have been preserved till now had not a neglected water-tank on the roof helped by its leakage the process of decay. The only vestiges of the building remaining are the old bricks, which pave the cellar floor of the present farm-house. The ancient house was sixty feet long and forty feet deep, with offices and adjoining buildings. It was begun in 1682, immediately upon Penn's arrival, and was constructed in the best style of the day, costing some thousands of pounds and consuming four or five years in its erection. With its stately porch in front and rear, and wide hall running through it, and spacious apartments, it must have presented an appearance of elegance unusual to the New World. There was stabling for twelve horses, and it was not forgotten to provide a brew-house in which to brew ale for the household.

A beautiful garden was laid out between the house and the river, and a broad shady walk added to the grace of these elegant grounds. In the years 1700 and 1701 the founder lived here in the style usual to men of his rank in colonial times, entertaining frequent guests with liberal hospitality. The Indians here held conference with the distinguished Friend, and on one occasion he gave a feast under the poplars at the manor to his Indian visitors, at which time one hundred turkeys were served up, "besides venison and other meats." In attending to his extensive plantations Penn was often away, so that he frequently passed in his barge from Philadelphia, then beginning its history, to this manor home on the Delaware, which was then wooded to its very edge with stately forest-trees. But he was not permitted long to enjoy his rural tastes. Interests imperilled by political changes called him to England, and though he hoped soon to return and spend the evening of his life in this chosen home, his wish was never gratified.

The country about and beyond Pennsbury Manor is classic ground. Not far away is the site of the house in which Moreau, Napoleon's old marshal and the victor of Hohenlinden, led the life of an American country gentleman until, in an evil hour, he listened to the proposals of the Emperors of Austria and Russia, and went back to Europe to have his legs shot off at Dresden; a short distance to the north Washington made his famous "crossing of the Delaware" on the Christmas Eve of 1776, a few miles to the south is Trappe, long the home of Muhlenberg, and an easy morning's journey through Bucks and Montgomery into Chester takes one to historic Valley Forge, where was passed the gloomiest and saddest period of the war for independence.

Trappe, which lies near the lower edge of Montgomery County, is a small place and modest, but it has played its part in history, for it was here, in 1733, that the first Lutheran place of worship in America was erected, and it was here that Muhlenberg began his great work of establishing the doctrine of his church in this country. He came from Germany to the settlement of Trappe in 1742, and found a structure of logs that the primitive Lutherans had built to worship in. In 1743 he built a stone church to take the place of the rude log sanctuary, and it stands to-day just as it was finished a century and a half ago. It has not been used for church service for many years, but is sacredly preserved for its historic associations.

The walls of this ancient church are moss-grown and worn by wind and storm, but they are firm, and able to defy decay and ruin for another century. Its odd and angular architecture is striking. There is no steeple, and from the peak the roof slopes gradually for a few feet, and then drops at a sharp angle to the eaves. The heavy arched vestibule door is fastened by a ponderous lock, the great key that unlocks it being yellow and eaten with rust.

The interior of the church is as it was the day services were first held in it by Muhlenberg, except that the high, straight-backed pews show the marks of occupancy by generations of worshippers. The curious oaken pulpit, hanging high against the wall at one end of the room, and reached by a long flight of steps, is the same from which Muhlenberg preached. Above the pulpit is the sounding-board that aided in making the preacher's words more distinct to his hearers.

A gallery of hewn oak timbers, with quaint wrought-iron braces to support it, extends around three sides of the room. Paint never stained the interior of the old church, and it was never heated, even in the coldest weather. Over the door on the outside a Latin inscription could once be read, but the rude letters have been so obliterated by time that they can no longer be deciphered.

The burial-ground of this ancient edifice contains the graves of the pioneers of Lutheranism in this country, and here repose the remains of Father Muhlenberg himself. Beside his lie those of his distinguished son, Peter, who was preacher, soldier, and statesman. It was this son who, at the breaking out of the Revolutionary War, appeared in the pulpit dressed in the uniform of a colonel, and telling his people that there was a time to preach and a time to fight, and the time had come to fight, proceeded to enlist men for the patriot army on the spot.

From Trappe, which promises to long remain one of the most delightful of New World nooks, a tree-embowered road winds southward between low hills to the site of

Washington's camp at Valley Forge. This covers some two thousand acres of rolling meadow-land, broken here and there with abrupt wooded hills. The old stone mansion occupied as head-quarters by Washington and his staff fronts the station of the Philadelphia and Reading Railroad. Southward, at a distance of a quarter of a mile, is the spot where Washington's original head-quarters stood, the building, now removed, which he occupied in December, 1777. A stone's throw from there is the bubbling spring known as "Washington's Spring," on the right bank of Valley Creek.

On the farther side of that stream, a step below, is the site of the old Valley Forge, from which the locality takes its name, built in 1757. To the southeast a few hundred yards, extending in a zigzag line north and south for a quarter of a mile, are the remains of the old entrenchments thrown up by the patriot troops, and still easily distinguished by the irregular and scattered heaps of stones and the uneven elevation of the greensward. To the right of these remains are the foundation-stones and de-

cayed timbers of Fort Washington, which
served as the eastern bulwark of the camp.
Southwest of this, a quarter of a mile farther, is the site of the head-quarters used
by Knox and the officers of his command,
and a short distance below, on the other
side of Valley Creek, is the site of Lafayette's head-quarters, a two-and-a-half story
house which still stands, little changed by
the years.

It was after the disastrous battles of the
Brandywine and Germantown that the Continental army went into camp at Valley
Forge. The enlisted men and their field
and line officers dwelt in cabins, each built
to accommodate twelve men. Six months
of terrible suffering were spent in these
dreary huts. The patriot troopers, ragged
and half starved, without shoes or blankets
or proper clothing, slept at night during the
whole dreadful winter of 1777-78 on the
bare earth, and in the daytime, in providing
firewood for their comfortless cabins, left
foot-tracks of blood on the frozen ground,
hallowing the very soil by the severity and
heroism of their sufferings. Disease added

its terrors to those of famine and cold, and smallpox wrought fearful havoc in the camp. Facilities of transportation were scarce, and such supplies as could be procured were carried upon the backs of the men and hauled in improvised hand-carts. By the middle of January, 1778, things were so desperate that General Varnum wrote to General Greene, " In all human probability the army must dissolve."

The prospect for American independence was dark indeed, but in the character of Washington was something which enabled him, notwithstanding the discordant materials of which his army was composed, and in spite of the hardships and privations his men endured, to so attach both officers and soldiers to his person that no distress could weaken their affections nor impair the respect and veneration in which he was held by them. When that army, after its trying ordeal, left Valley Forge, it started upon a career of victory, and never again knew the sting and bitterness of defeat. The battle of the Brandywine was the high-water mark of British success, and after June 18, 1777, until the surrender at Yorktown the army of the invader constantly met with reverses.

The passage of sixscore years has made few changes at Valley Forge. Trees have been cut down and the woods which sheltered Washington's soldiers have disappeared, but the generals' head-quarters, with one or two exceptions, are still standing, and the Potts mansion, which housed Washington and his staff and is now the property of the Sons of America, appears inside and out almost precisely as it was when occupied by the patriot captain.

A plain, somewhat contracted-looking house is this Valley Forge shrine, after the usual type of ancient Pennsylvania homesteads, with a queer roof over the door and narrow, small-paned windows that end in low, deep window-seats. Interest in the house centres in the back room used by Washington as a private office and furnished with articles gathered here and there of the date of Washington's residence, but the dwelling as a whole strikes the visitor as a bare-looking and somewhat dreary

85

place, and when its few relics have been inspected one is not unwilling to leave it for the drive over quiet country roads to the church built in 1715 and known as "Old St. David's at Radnor."

This little temple in the wilderness, of which Longfellow wrote in one of his last poems,—

> "What an image of peace and rest
>   Is this little church among its graves !
> All is so quiet ; the troubled breast,
> The wounded spirit, the heart oppressed,
>   Here may find the repose it craves.
>
> "See how the ivy climbs and expands
>   Over this humble hermitage,
> And seems to caress with its little hands
> The rough gray stones as a child that stands
>   Caressing the wrinkled cheeks of age.
>
> "You cross the threshold, and dim and small
>   Is the space that serves for the Shepherd's fold ;
> The narrow aisle, the bare, white wall,
> The pews and the pulpit, quaint and tall,
>   Whisper and say : 'Alas ! we are old !' "

stands in a secluded spot, among sloping fields and wooded hills, and wears an air of antiquity so marked that one might almost imagine himself transported to another age

OLD ST. DAVID'S, RADNOR, PENNSYLVANIA.

and country. The ivy-clad structure is of rough graystone, in the old Pennsylvania style. The walls are thick, the shingled roof low, the windows arched, and the shutters iron-barred. Within the church an oaken table serves for an altar, and the pews are square and provided with doors. A high gallery extends across the end, and this is reached by a flight of stone steps from the outside,—a peculiarity that forms one of its distinguishing features.

The little church stands in a forest of gravestones, and even its door-step covers the dust of one of the forefathers of Radnor, a certain William Moore, who, dying in 1781, was, it is said, buried beneath the step as a mark of dishonor, on account of his being a Tory. Another tale has it that this was a token of respect. He requested that his remains might be interred under the pulpit, and as the vestry were unwilling to place them within the church, it was decided that the suppliant's bones should be deposited in the next best location,—before the door. Be this as it may, Moore's memorial stone has been trodden upon for a hundred years,

so that his epitaph has become a blur,—little
of him to-day can be read but his name.

The most interesting spot in this fruitful
God's Acre is the grave of that fearless soldier of the Revolution, General Anthony
Wayne, who here takes his rest with his
wife and kindred beside him. A stately
monument marks the spot where his bones
were interred, in 1809, having been brought,
a dozen years after his death, from their
original resting-place at Erie to be deposited
amid the familiar scenes of his youth and
manhood. This second funeral was a great
event in the neighborhood. "The remains
of General Wayne," says the historian of
Old St. David's, "were removed from the
fortress at Presqu' Isle to Radnor church-
yard by his son, Colonel Isaac Wayne, and
at the same time (July 4, 1809) the Pennsylvania State Society of the Cincinnati, with
due ritual ceremonies, placed over the grave
of the illustrious dead the present monument.
The wonders of that day are still fresh in
the minds of some of our church-members;
the First City Troop, of Philadelphia, under
command of Mayor Robert Wharton, rode

out to Radnor, and performed the honors of war over the grave of the general, but so excessively hot was the day that one of the officers is said to have fainted while coming down the hill near which the present parsonage stands. The hearse proceeded from Mr. Wayne's house to the church, and an old soldier named Samuel Smiley is said to have marched before it all the way, refusing to ride, and mourning the loss of his old commander."

There is another noble reminder of Wayne in the land which holds his dust. Just over the hills from Old St. David's is the house in which he was born, and where he spent most of his life when not engaged in military campaigns,—a grand old homestead, still owned and occupied by his descendants. The house is filled with relics of Wayne, and the parlor is furnished exactly as it was in the general's time. It has an antique fireplace, with brass andirons and fender, and on the mantel are two pairs of china vases with handles that have survived without a crack, and a pair of silver candlesticks and snuffers. A beautiful old mirror fills the space between the windows, the stiff draperies of the period that cross it from the window almost concealing its beauty. These draperies are looped with gilt pins, and harmonize thoroughly with the ancient-looking sofa and chairs and the stiff neutral-hued carpet. The chairs, of course, are high-backed and broad-seated, after the fashion of a century ago, and the room as a whole is an admirable relic of that olden time.

A leisurely half-hour's stroll from the Wayne homestead is Paoli, scene of the massacre of a hundred and fifty American soldiers on the night of September 20, 1777,—nine days after the battle of the Brandywine. The Americans, pursued by the British, had fallen back to Warwick Furnace, in Chester County, and General Wayne, whose command numbered some fifteen hundred men, had been ordered by Washington to cut off the enemy's baggage-train and halt his advance towards Schuylkill valley, thus affording the Continentals time to cross the river and march down the other side.

Wayne moved quickly, and the afternoon of September 20 found him encamped near the spot now marked by the Paoli monument, some four miles in the rear of the British army. It was his purpose to attack the enemy's rear whenever they should resume their march towards the Schuylkill, but he did not take into account the treachery of his old friends and neighbors. Late that night, under cover of darkness and guided by Tory residents of the countryside, the British general, Grey, massed his troops as near the camp of Wayne as possible without betraying a knowledge of his approach through the woods, and made a deadly charge upon the American corps.

Although cleverly executed, the surprise was not complete. The assailants were received with several close and destructive volleys which must have done great execution; but the Americans were greatly outnumbered, and, in the end, were obliged to retreat in haste and disorder. Many victims were massacred after resistance on their part had ceased; the cry for quarter was unheeded, and the British bayonet did its work with unpitying ferocity. Of the American dead, fifty-three were laid in one grave. A pile of stones marked their burial-spot until 1817, when a monument was placed above it by the people of Chester. The present monument, a handsome granite shaft, with inscriptions on the four sides, was unveiled on the centennial of the massacre in 1877.

Paoli, which borrows its name from the Corsican general Pasquale di Paoli, leader of the revolt against the Genoese, is an old, old place in the midst of charming scenery; and, indeed, full of legend and story, as are nearly all the beautiful nooks and hamlets of Southeastern Pennsylvania. There is Swarthmore, with its memories of Benjamin West; and there are the Quaker villages of Kennett Square, Oxford, and Calvert; Robert Fulton's birthplace among the Conowingo Hills, and sleepy Manheim, on the hitherside of Lancaster, with its stories of Baron Stiegel and its yearly "Feast of the Roses,"—all within compass of a day's journey by rail or wheel from Philadelphia.

Swarthmore, the Springfield of other days, was founded by Thomas Pierson, the friend and comrade of William Penn. Thomas Pierson's daughter married John

West, and one of the children of this union was Benjamin West, the painter. West left America when he was twenty-two years old never to return, but the house in which he was born, a stone structure with dormer-windows set squarely in the sloping roof, still stands inside the college grounds at Swarthmore very like it was in the painter's youth. Here, with no guide save native love for the beautiful, West began to draw and paint, and the first expression of his talent was in the picture of a sleeping child, drawn in this old house. It is commonly told that it was his sleeping sister who inspired him; but Benjamin was the youngest of his father's children. The mother of the baby was Benjamin's sister. She had come with the infant to spend a few days with her parents. When the child was asleep, Mrs. West invited the mother to gather flowers in the garden, giving the little boy a fan with which to flap away the flies while he watched the baby in their absence.

The child smiled in its sleep. Seizing pen and paper, and having fortunately both red and black ink on a table near by, he drew

a picture which he endeavored to conceal
when his mother and sister entered. The
mother, noticing his confusion, requested
him to show what he was hiding. Mrs.
West looked at the drawing with pleasure,
and said to her daughter, " I declare, he has
made a likeness of little Sally," and kissed
him with fondness and satisfaction. This
is chronicled in Galt's " Life of Benjamin
West" as " the birth of fine art in the New
World."

The old house at Swarthmore also brings
to mind the piquant romance of which West
was the hero. Elizabeth Shewell was an
orphan girl residing with her brother in
Philadelphia. This brother, an ambitious
man, urged her to marry a wealthy suitor,
but she refused, having already pledged her
vows to West. Thereafter a close watch
was kept upon the girl, and orders given
to the servants to refuse admittance to West
if he ever came to the door. ·For five
years Elizabeth waited; then assisted by
friends, watching within and without,—
Benjamin Franklin was one of them,—she
descended a rope-ladder from the window

of her room, and was hurried into a waiting carriage and driven rapidly to the wharf, where a ship was ready to sail. The father of West received her, cared for her during the voyage, and delivered her to the eager lover, who came aboard the ship at Liverpool and embraced her rapturously.

"Hast thou no welcome for thy old father, Benjamin?" asked the aged Quaker, who stood, smiling, to behold their joyful meeting.

"That I have, father!" cried the son, and the father never after felt a moment's neglect.

The lovers, upon their arrival in London, went at once to St. Martin's-in-the-Fields, a favorite church for weddings to this day, and marriage sealed a union which never knew discord or sorrow. West, in afteryears, sent a portrait of his wife as a peaceoffering to her brother, who never looked at it, but had it stowed away in the garret of his house. One of his grandchildren remembers having beaten with a switch the portrait of his "naughty aunty" who smiled upon the children playing in the attic, where she

had gone to weep, a lovelorn maiden,—
smiled upon them from her calm estate of
wedded bliss in England.

Swarthmore lies midway between Paoli
and the Delaware, and from it a railroad
runs to Kennett Square, another quaint
Quaker village, now indissolubly bound up
with the name and fame of Bayard Taylor.
This poet was born and spent his early youth
in or near Kennett Square, and when he had
won fame and fortune he realized a dream
that had haunted him in his travels and, in
1859, built Cedarcraft, a dignified mansion
placed in the midst of a broad domain about
a mile from the town of Kennett and facing
the home of his youth. Nearing it from the
village, one catches a glimpse of the house
through the trees that cluster about it, but,
as one drives or walks on, it is soon shut from
view by a grove of oaks and chestnuts that
rise like a wall on the hither side of the estate. A low hill ascended, one comes to a
wide rustic gate, which opens into a short
woodland drive, at the end of which stands
the house, kept in excellent condition by its
present owner.

A substantial, two-storied structure of red brick, with corners of gray granite, Cedarcraft has a spacious and a cosy look, such as a poet's home ought to have. Taylor loved it as he did no other spot on earth, and within its walls he did the greater part of his best work, for it was at Cedarcraft that he wrote " The Poet's Journal," " The Masque of the Gods," " Home Pastorals," and " Deukalion," his two novels, " Joseph and his Friends" and " The Story of Kennett," and the major portion of his translation of " Faust,"—the crowning literary effort of his life.

Taylor left Cedarcraft for the last time in the summer of 1877. He died a few months later in Berlin, whither he had gone as United States minister. In March, 1879, his body was brought back to America and laid to rest in Longwood Cemetery, a few miles from Kennett, where a modest monument marks the graves of the poet and of his first wife, Mary Agnew. But it is Cedarcraft that is and will long remain Taylor's most speaking memorial. Its owner should count himself a fortunate man, for in possessing it he possesses more than his house and his grounds,—the home in which a famous and gifted poet once lived, and which will always be associated with his memory,—a shrine to which reverent pilgrimages will be made in the years to come.

Kennett Square, a handful of houses lying along clean roadways, remains as in Taylor's time a distinctively Quaker community, and Oxford and Calvert, to the west and south of it, are still given over in the main to members of the Society of Friends. Calvert, settled in 1701, and known until very recently as Brick Meeting-House, is the oldest of the three, and most of its people dwell on lands given to their forefathers by William Penn. Thrift rules in Calvert, and abstinence and prudence regulate its morals. The inhabitants under protest pay tribute to the State and Federal governments and a subsidy to support a national army. Moreover, there is the tradition of a long-gone day, what time the whole country thrilled with martial music and the tread of soldiers marching to the battles of the Civil War, that came freighted with dire import for peaceful Calvert, whose simple souls as yet realized but dimly that war had the nation by its throat.

On the day noted, however, a government tax-gatherer invaded the community in the interest of his duty to lay a war tax there, and a tranquil-minded patriarch, the wealthiest and most influential citizen of the village, impelled by his resolute scruples against warfare, persistently refused to pay his individual assessment. He placidly accompanied an officer of the law to the shire town and was lodged in the county jail, where, sustained by his conscience, he bore imprisonment with meekness and fortitude. After he had been confined there a week or more a wealthy citizen of another faith paid the Quaker's war tax, and the old man went back to his home and hill-side acres.

Since then Calvert has been a hamlet without a history, a domain given over to peace, where Time's course is as smooth as a June breeze in the meadows. Peaceful and benignant, yet retiring and self-contained, the Quakers of Calvert seldom, if ever, seek converts among the people about them, but on each First Day they faithfully gather at the Old Brick Meeting-House, one of the Friends' most widely known landmarks, within the walls of which seven generations have worshipped after the fashion taught by Fox and Penn, and attendance at one of their meetings proves an experience not likely to be soon forgotten. When all the seats are filled there is stillness for a time, and then the voice of some Friend "moved by the spirit" will be heard. Beginning in ordinary tones, the utterance soon rises to the peculiar sing-song of the sect,—fascinating and appropriate when used by some sweet-voiced woman Friend, but grating not a little on worldly ears when in the nasal twang of some fervent male exhorter. This finished, perhaps some one will offer prayer. Now and then a member whom the spirit has never moved before will get up, speak a few words, and sit down. It is seldom that more than two or three speak. A clasp of hands across the low partition, which divides the meeting-room into two parts, by the man and woman nearest each other on the front seat ends the service, and with the rustle of the women's dresses and the noisier footfalls of the worshippers follows the quick emptying of the house.

Calvert was settled, as I have said, in 1701, and the burial-ground around the Old Brick Meeting-House is now thickly sown with the graves of the hamlet's dead. One of these mounds covers the dust of a woman whose career offers a tempting theme for the story-teller. Elizabeth Maxwell was a comely and spirited English maiden, born in the opening year of the eighteenth century. Her mother and her uncle, Daniel Defoe,— the same Daniel Defoe who wrote "Robinson Crusoe" and "The Plague in London," —frowned upon the attentions paid her by a young man in London, and eighteen-year-old Elizabeth, angered by their treatment, left home secretly and suddenly and took passage on a vessel for the New World.

The wilful girl, having no money with which to pay her passage, agreed with the captain, as was common in those days, to be sold for a term of years on reaching America. The sale occurred in Philadelphia in the fall of 1718, a number of other persons who came across the sea in like manner being offered at the same time. Andrew Job, of Calvert, attended the sale, purchased Elizabeth for a period of years, and took her to his home, where Thomas Job, his kinsman, fell in love with and married her. After her marriage she wrote her relatives in London of her circumstances and surroundings. Her uncle, Daniel Defoe, replied that her mother had died and left property by will to her. A list of the property came with the letter, and her uncle was desirous that she should take especial care of articles he had used in his study, "as they had descended to the family from their Flemish ancestors, who sought refuge under the banner of Queen Elizabeth from the tyranny of Philippe." Among the goods sent over were two chairs he had used in his study, and which are still in the keeping of his niece's descendants. Mrs. Job dwelt happily in Calvert until her death in 1782.

Fulton's birthplace is a few miles west of Oxford, in what was formerly Little Britain township, — now Fulton, — in Lancaster County. The house in which the inventor was born is of stone, plastered outside, two stories high, and one end of the long, low structure is higher than the other. At the east end is a small porch set under the overhanging roof. The side of the house, which is, perhaps, fifty feet long, is near the foot of a sunny hill-slope, and through the hollow runs the Conowingo Creek, which empties into the Susquehanna. A large white modest barn is behind the dwelling, and a rusty, narrow-gauge railroad runs before the side yard, at the crossing of a dusty clay road.

When Fulton was born in 1765, the house was used as a tavern, and it is said that his father, an Irishman from Kilkenny, was the proprietor of it for a number of years. The elder Fulton fell into financial straits, and, in 1772, his home passed to the ownership of Joseph Swift, of Philadelphia, in the possession of whose descendants it has remained to this day. This corner of Lancaster County has produced many eminent men. David Ramsay, the historian of South Carolina, was born in Drumore township, near Fulton House, and Oliver Evans, who is said to have made the first traction engine for common roads, came into life on the Red Clay Creek, which flows only a few miles from Fulton's birthplace.

Before he was twenty Fulton left Lancaster County never to return, but as a child playing about the doorway of his father's tavern he no doubt often saw Baron Stiegel sweep by on the way from Philadelphia to his country-seats at Manheim and Shaefferstown. Stiegel was the hero of an exceptional career. Descended from a wealthy and titled German family, he came to America in 1750 and became one of the pioneer ironmasters and glass manufacturers in the colonies. His furnace was at Elizabeth and his glass factory at Manheim. The baron resided in Philadelphia, where he had married an American wife, and his frequent journeys to his iron- and glass-works were imposing affairs. The coach in which he rode was drawn by four, and sometimes eight, horses. Postilions were ever at hand, and hounds ran ahead of the horses.

The reception accorded the baron on these visits by his workmen and retainers was a

lordly one. At the first sight of his approach the watchman in the cupola of the
mansion he had erected at Manheim fired a
cannon, which told the inhabitants their
master was coming. The citizens and a
band of musicians moved to the residence.
Into town the baron swept, and was wel-
comed with cheers, music, and cannon. The
cannon at Manheim was heard at Elizabeth
Furnace, twelve miles away, and preparations were made to receive him. On leaving
Manheim a salute was fired, and the furnace
people knew he was on his way. Near Elizabeth there was a high hill, on which a cannon
was placed, and at the first sight of the
baron's carriage a shot was fired. The workmen in the furnace ceased their labors and,
taking up their music, prepared to receive
their master. From the furnace he would
drive to Shaefferstown, where he had erected
a large tower, on which was a cannon. This
tower, since destroyed, was erected for the
purpose of entertaining therein his intimate
friends, and contained several apartments.

For the better part of a generation Stiegel
was the wealthiest resident of the colony, ex-

cept the Penns. But his wealth was not un-
limited nor his business foresight altogether
perfect. He lived quite beyond his means
and failed. He even was imprisoned for
debt. Before the Revolution cut off his re-
sources in Europe a special act was passed
for his relief. But he never recovered. His
towers stood as the castles of folly, and his
former luxury mocked him. He died in ob-
scurity when he filled no higher position than
that of a village schoolmaster.

However, his memory is kept alive at
Manheim by his former residence, which
now forms a part of one of the business
houses of the town, and by a yearly function
as unique as it is beautiful. When, in 1772,
the baron gave the Lutherans of Manheim
land on which to build a church, he stipu-
lated that the annual rent should be "one red
rose in the month of June forever." Every
year this rental rose is paid to the oldest of
Stiegel's descendants, and the ceremony attending its payment has come to be known as
the "Feast of the Roses." Until its observance lapses the name and fame of the eccentric baron will remain unforgotten.

CHAPTER XI

IMAGINE a dingy, straggling, unpaved town, shut in by surrounding hills and by a low line of mountains, a town which stopped growing early in the century, and whose weather-beaten dwellings and other buildings show that it has been many a day since there has been work for the carpenter and painter to do, and one will have a fair idea of the Dunker village of Ephrata, which lies twenty miles by rail from Lancaster, Pennsylvania, and impresses one with the singular sense of being a place in which something is always about to happen, but nothing ever does happen in it, or ever will. Quieter it could not be, unless it were absolutely dead. The stranger let down by chance in Ephrata might easily imagine himself in a peasant village of South Germany, for its founders came from Witsgenstein, and although it is more than one hundred and fifty years since they built their huts of log and stone and took up the hard, laborious lives of New World pioneers, their descendants are still faithful to the traditions and customs, and in many instances to the vernacular of the fatherland.

The founders of the curious sect, whose members now own and till the fertile acres about Ephrata, were first heard of in Germany early in the eighteenth century. Only three confessions, the Catholics, the Lutherans, and the Calvinists, under the laws of the empire, were then allowed free exercise of their religious worship; all others being counted unsound, erratic, and dangerous, yet in a few secluded and scattered nooks the Separatists found not only an asylum but, through the sympathy of the rulers, a cordial welcome. This was the case in the territories of the Counts of Isenberg and Wittgenstein, where in 1708 a little group of Separatists under the lead of Alexander Mack, a miller of Schriesheim, resolved " to establish a covenant of conscience, and to accept the teachings of Christ as a gentle yoke," solemnizing their union by immersion in the river Eder, near Schwarzenau. Such was the origin of the Dunkers, whose founders numbered less than half a score, but soon received considerable accessions from the Palatinate, Würtemberg, and Switzerland. Prompted by this increase in numbers, a branch was established at Marienborn, in the principality of Isenberg, but the halcyon days of the infant sect were followed by scattering storms.

In 1715 the members of the Marienborn society removed to Crefeld, and four years later to the number of two hundred sought an asylum in Pennsylvania, settling mainly at Germantown near Philadelphia, where they organized a congregation in 1723. In 1729 the members of the present society at Schwarzenau followed the example of their brethren and emigrated to America. With the lapse of the years the Dunkers spread into the interior counties of Pennsylvania, and the yearly conference, dealing with the common concerns of the sect, was, in the course of time, alternately held east and west of the Susquehanna River. Gradually they found their way into Maryland, Virginia, North Carolina, and the Western States of Ohio and Indiana, and now in every second year the conference is held west of the Ohio, while Kansas, Nebraska, the Dakotas, Colorado, Idaho, California, Oregon, and Washington have their Dunker congregations. At the present time God's Peculiar People, as the Dunkers delight to call themselves, number in the United States—for they also have missions in Europe—about two hundred thousand souls, with some two thousand ministers to attend to their spiritual wants, none of whom receives a salary.

The creed of the Dunkards is a naif and simple one. "Be it known unto all men," writes one of its exponents and defenders, "that there is a people who, as little children, accept the word of the New Testament as a message from heaven and teach it in full. They baptize believers by triune immersion, with a forward action, and for the remission of sins, and lay hands on those baptized, asking upon them the gift of God's spirit. They follow the command and example of washing one another's feet. They take the Lord's Supper at night at one and the same time, tarrying one for another.

They greet one another with a holy kiss. They teach all the doctrines of Christ, peace, love, unity, both faith and works. They labor for nonconformity to the world in its vain and wicked customs. They advocate non-swearing, anti-secretism, opposition to war, and doing good to all men. They anoint and lay hands on the sick. They give the bread of life, the message of the common salvation, unto all men without money or price. For the above we contend earnestly, and all men are entreated to hear, examine, and accept it as the word which began to be spoken by the Lord, and the faith that was delivered to the saints."

The dress and customs of the Dunkers are as primitive as their creed. The men let their beards grow and part their flowing hair in the middle, and wear slouch hats and the plainest of clothes. The garb of the women is equally plain and severe. There are no milliners among them, for each woman makes her own hat, a simple matter, since no feathers or other ornamentation is allowed, while the wearing of jewelry is strictly forbidden. However, the Dunker women are seldom wanting in comeliness. Their faces are nearly always sweet and gentle, while an air of almost saintly simplicity is given them by the clear-starched cap, the handkerchief crossed on the breast, the white apron, and the plain gray or drab stuff of their dresses. The Dunkers live in peace one with another, and never have recourse to law to redress an injury done to them. Disputes among themselves are settled by the elders, whose decision is final, and only in exceptional cases do they institute lawsuits against the people of the world. They are averse to accepting public office, and rarely, if ever, exercise the right of franchise. However, the Dunker ideal of personal conduct is a high one. They are temperate to abstemiousness, industrious and economical, and Carlyle's gospel of work is theirs. They allow no public money to be expended for their poor or helpless, but provide for them among themselves, and their two hundred thousand members do not include any one who suffers from want. Even those who fail in business are aided to make a new effort, and such assistance may be lent three times. After the third failure, they accept it as the will of God that the unfortunate brother shall not succeed, and thenceforth the aid given him takes another form.

Naifly primitive is the Dunker celebration of the Lord's Supper. It is observed in the evening, and is always preceded in the afternoon by a love-feast. This commemorates the supper which Jesus took with His disciples, and is a solemn religious festivity, each Dunker church having its kitchen provided with great kettles and plain dishes for its proper observance. When the occasion is at hand, after a day of preaching, a lamb is killed and a clear soup is made, into which bread is broken, and then served in great bowls placed on long and very narrow tables, at each side of which sit the participants, four persons eating from each bowl. After the eating of the broth comes the ceremony known as the washing of feet, each sex performing this duty for its own. Those who are to engage in the ordinance presently enter the meeting, carrying tubs of lukewarm water, and each member on the front benches removes his or her shoes and stockings. A man on the men's side and a woman on the women's side then wash the feet one by one, taking the right hand of each individual as they finish the washing, and giving the kiss of peace. As one benchful has the ceremony performed, it gives place to another, the minister or teachers meanwhile making a brief speech or reading appropriate portions of Scripture relating to the subject.

Following this ceremony comes the supper itself. Each third bench is so arranged that the back can be turned upon a pivot at each end, so as to form the top of a long table. This is covered with a white cloth, and presently brothers and sisters enter, bearing large bowls of soup, plates of bread and meat, and pies and coffee. Three or four people help themselves out of the same dish, and the ceremony known as the salutation of the holy kiss concludes the supper. Each brother imparts a hearty kiss on the bearded lips of his neighbor at table, and in the same manner each sister kisses her sister companion sitting nearest to her. The communion service which follows consists in the breaking of unleavened bread and the drinking of unfermented wine, the whole ceremony being concluded by the singing of hymns and preaching. This the Dunkers contend is the only true method of administering the ordinance of the Last Supper, and also hold that it is an exact and faithful copy of that ceremony as celebrated in the earliest Christian Church. Not less interesting than the foregoing is the Dunker ordinance of anointing the sick with oil. The sick one calls upon the elders of the meeting, and at a settled time the ceremony is performed. It consists of pouring oil upon the head of the sick person, and of laying hands upon and praying over him.

Dunker or Tunker comes from the German tunker, which means to dip, and rigid adherence is still given to the doctrine laid down by Mack, that no soul can hope to enter the realms of the blest unless the body has been plunged three times face downward into the water. Nor is the method ever modified by stress of weather. It is not uncommon in the winter to see a party of stalwart Dunkers chopping through six or eight inches of ice in order to clear a space in which to immerse the faithful, who piously pray

God to "write their names in the Book of Life," and I shall long remember a Dunker dipping of which I was a witness on a bitter January day several years ago. It occurred at a spring on the farm of a Dunker named Hostetter, who lives not far from Ephrata. There was little delay after those who were expected had arrived, and soon the demure procession left the farm-house for the spring. The three men who were about to make public profession of their faith by dipping in the icy water wore only their shirts, trousers, and shoes, and were closely muffled up in buffalo-robes. The four women—three of them were buxom maidens and the other a gray-haired matron—were clad in loose gowns of some coarse material, and were also muffled in blankets, shawls, and robes.

When the spring was reached the Dunker faithful formed a circle on the edge of the stream and Preacher Amos Holtenstein offered a prayer, invoking the Divine blessing upon the water. Then the preacher, who had a long stick in his hand, waded into the water. He felt around with his cane until he came to what appeared to be a favorable

spot, when he indicated that he was ready
to receive the first candidate for dipping.
Preacher Jesse Sonan led a young man to
the edge of the brook. His bronzed cheeks
seemed to have a heightened color and a
bright light shone in his eye, but his evident
determination did not prevent the shiver that
passed over him as his legs came in contact
with the cold water, and his teeth chattered
as he returned his replies to the solemn questions of the preacher. The first thing the
latter did was to throw water over the shoulders, neck, and that part of the young man's
body not covered by the stream, in order that
no portion should remain untouched. Then
the questions were asked and answered in
Pennsylvania Dutch, and the supreme moment came when Preacher Holtenstein pronounced the solemn formula, " In namen der
Dreinichte, Fader, Sohn und Heilichen
Geist." At each mention of the name of the
Deity the preacher plunged the head of the
young man beneath the water face downward. Then, while the man knelt in the
water, the preacher prayed that his name
might be written in the Book of Life, a kiss

upon the cheek concluding the ceremony. Exactly the same form was observed with the six other candidates, save that whereas the preacher kissed the men, he did not kiss the women.

A singular feature of the occasion was the seeming insensibility to the cold shown by Preacher Holtenstein, who though in the water for upward of an hour appeared to suffer no discomfort. In answer to a question, he said reverently that he knew the Lord gave him strength and upheld those who were thus baptized in winter weather, quaintly adding, " I have baptized more than three hundred in just such weather as this and not one died." Preacher Holtenstein, it may be observed in passing, is an admirable example of the Dunker minister, who is chosen from the laity by the members of the church, he who receives the largest number of votes being pronounced elected. These elections are summoned by the elders of the church, who preside over them and receive the votes of the people, either *viva voce,* in whispers, or by closed ballots. The successful candidate is expected to support himself,—he is usually a prosperous farmer, —and, as already stated, receives nothing for his labors as a shepherd to his flock. Under these conditions, as might be expected, a man loses something of effectiveness in the pulpit, and the Dunker preacher's sermons are usually expositions of the peculiar doctrines of his sect. They seem, however, to be a means of grace to those who listen to them and to breed an enviable fibre of endurance.

There have been from time to time more or less important secessions from the Dunker Church, and of the strangest, most remarkable of these Ephrata boasts the mute yet eloquent reminders in a curious pile of buildings of odd, old-fashioned architecture, which were once the home and habitat of Conrad Beissel's singular Order of the Solitary. Beissel, who learned the trade of weaver under Peter Becker, the first Dunker preacher in this country, was a man of intelligence and education. Accepting the idea of primitive Christianity inculcated by the Dunkers, he saw no reason why they should stop short of complete reformation and return to the principles of apostolic times in respect to observing the seventh instead of the first day of the week as the Sabbath. Upon this subject he wrote a tract, which he published in 1728. This created great disturbance among the Dunkers and led to numerous withdrawals from the society, Beissel himself retiring to a cave at the future site of Ephrata on the banks of the Cocalico and taking up the life of a recluse. Here he was joined by many of his old friends, together with others who, made converts by his tracts, settled in the neighborhood of his once solitary habitation.

At the end of four years this recluse life was changed to a monastic one, and in 1735 the first cenobitic building, called Kedar, was put up in the centre of the village, to which Beissel, in allusion to the 132d Psalm, had given the name of Ephrata. It contained a large room for religious exercise, halls for love-feasts and feet-washing, and several cells for solitary brethren and sisters, the latter occupying the second story. Monastic names were given to all who entered it, the prior, Israel Echerlin, taking the name of

Onesimus, and Beissel, who steadily refused to accept any position of influence, that of Friedsam, together with the title of Spiritual Father of the community. No vows of celibacy were exacted or taken, but the idea was considerably inculcated, while the habit of the Capuchins, or White Friars, was early adopted by the members of the new society. The brothers wore shirt, trousers, and vests, with a long white gown and cowl, and the costume of the sisters was the same, with the exception of a coarse flannel petticoat substituted for the trousers and the addition of a large veil reaching front and back to the girdle, and resembling a scapulary. The garments used in winter were of wool, and in summer of linen and cotton. Both sexes went barefooted during the warm season.

From time to time other buildings, designed to serve religious, residential, or industrial purposes, were added to the Kloster. In 1738 a large house, called Zion, was built; another, Peniel, went up in 1741, and in 1745 Saron, one of the buildings still standing, was erected as a convent for self-divorced couples, the men and the women living in different parts of the house. The plan, however, would not work. The letters of divorce were torn up by mutual consent; the couples returned to their homesteads, and Saron was assigned to the sisters. New quarters being required for the monks, Bethania was built in 1746, with accommodations for one hundred solitary brethren. The Kloster, which now included some three hundred persons, had been from the first a hive of industry. There were no idlers, and work was found for all on the farm, where at first the brethren themselves took the place of horses and oxen at the plough; in the mills, at a trade, in the copying-room, in the printing-office or the bindery. There was no end of building, and all the labor was done by members of the society, which thus made itself independent of the outside world. Its mills were for many years the most extensive in the colony, embracing flour-, paper-, saw-, and fulling-mills, of which few traces now remain, while at Ephrata was erected in 1742 one of the first printing-presses set up in Pennsylvania, on it being printed most of the books and tracts of the society, which are

SAAL AND SARON, EPHRATA, PENNSYLVANIA.

now eagerly sought after by bibliophiles. Its wealth was for many years the common stock of the society, the income being devoted to the common support, and those who applied for membership being compelled to surrender all they had, absolutely and without reserve. Thus, more than a century before Proudhon ventured upon the bold paradox that property is theft, his doctrine had been taught and practised by Beissel and his followers.

Not the least singular among the singular customs of the Kloster were the love-feasts and the night services. The former were held now and then at the houses of affiliated brethren, but most often in the halls of the convent, sometimes for one sex, at other times for both. The night services were held whenever Beissel, or Father Friedsam, as he was called by his followers, gave the summons. This he occasionally did without previous announcement by pulling at a bell-cord that stretched from his dwelling to the male and female cloisters, whereupon, no matter what the hour, all had to dress and hasten to the meeting-place. Like the Dunkers from whom they had seceded, Beissel and his adherents regarded the strict and literal interpretation of the Bible as the only rule of faith. · They administered apostolic baptism with triune immersion, laying on hands and praying while the recipient still knelt in the water, and they celebrated the Lord's Supper at night, greeting one another with a kiss and washing each other's feet.

Conventual life at Ephrata was of the severest kind. The cells were only twenty inches wide and five feet high, and a bench, with a billet of wood for the head, was the couch of each inmate, while the corridors were so narrow that two persons could not pass, and if a chance meeting occurred, one had to back to the opening of a cell and stand in the niche until the other had passed. The fare of the inmates was fruit and vegetables, and they ate from wooden plates and drank from wooden goblets. Beissel, who was an accomplished musician, composed all the hymns sung at the gatherings of the society and trained several female choirs, whose singing is described by those who heard it as being exceptionally sweet and tender. " The performers," writes one visitor in a letter to Governor Penn, " sat with their heads reclined, their countenances solemn and dejected, their faces pale and emaciated from their manner of living, the clothing exceeding white and quite picturesque, and their music such as thrilled the very soul. I almost began to think myself in the world of spirits." Many of Beissel's manuscript hymns—he is said to have composed upward of four hundred airs—are still preserved in and about Ephrata. Some of them are marvels of beauty and artistic penmanship, the result of months, mayhap years, of toil by those who copied them, and would be a prize for the antiquarian, could access be gained to them.

Tradition has it that the copyist most skilful in transcribing Beissel's manuscripts was Sister Tabea, a Swiss girl of beautiful face and figure, who before she joined the Society of the Solitary had been known to the world as Margaret Thome. There were those who said that she was of too lively a disposition to end her days in nun's garb. At any rate,

when Daniel Scheible began to send her love-
letters she failed to inform those in authority
of this breach of rule, for who ever knew of
a maid displeased with proofs of the affection
of a personable youth? The parents of Sister Tabea's lover had been Dunkers who had
sought an asylum in America by taking ship
for Philadelphia, agreeing to be sold for a
term of years to pay for the fare. They
died on the passage, and their son was sold
for the rest of his minority to cancel their
unpaid debt. As a promising boy he had
been bought by the Ephrata brotherhood
and bred into the fraternity, where, with the
audacity of youth, he conceived a great passion for Sister Tabea, sending her any number of surreptitious notes, in which he set
forth the golden future within their reach
provided she would marry and go away with
him to Philadelphia, where he was planning,
now that his apprenticeship was about to ex-
pire, to seek his fortune.

At first Sister Tabea paid no heed to these
tender missives; then she sent an answer to
one of them, and in the end, after many fluc-
tuations in mind, she promised Scheible to

forsake the convent for the joys of a home. The day of the wedding was fixed by means of the notes which she continued to secretly exchange with Scheible, and she prepared to leave Saron and Ephrata for good and all. But when she went to take leave of Beissel her resolution failed her. Deep in the inmost recesses of her heart she had all along loved Brother Friedsam more fondly than she did all other men, and now bursting into tears, she declared that she had denied the Lord, and begged for permission to renew her vows to the society. This was given her, and Scheible, after vainly trying to persuade her to redeem the pledge she had given to him, took solitary and sorrowful leave of Ephrata, nor did the little village ever see him more. The next Saturday, for the seventh day was the Ephrata Sabbath, Tabea took a new, solemn, and irrevocable vow; and from that hour until the day of her death she was called Sister Anastasia,—the name signifying that she had been reëstablished. What source of consolation she had her companions never divined, for how should they guess that alongside her religious fervor grew a tender and self-nurtured human love. And I doubt if Brother Friedsam ever suspected the truth.

He died in 1768, and his spiritual leadership devolved upon Peter Miller, who for many years had been prior of the order, and was a man of great learning and saintly life. He was, moreover, an ardent patriot, and during the Revolution won and held the friendship of many of the leaders, including Washington. The story of one of Miller's meetings with the latter demands a place in this chronicle. One Michael Widman, an innkeeper of the countryside and a stanch member of the Dunker Church, had conceived a spiteful feeling against Miller because he had renounced the Dunker creed to join the Ephrata brotherhood. When abusive language failed to ruffle Miller's temper, Widman went so far as to spit in his face without provoking to anger the meek and gentle head of the Order of the Solitary. Time, however, brought an opportunity for revenge: during the Revolution Widman acted as a spy for the British, an offence that when he fell into the hands of the Americans brought him under a sentence of death. News of his impending fate soon reached Ephrata, and was received with unanimous approval. Not quite unanimous, for there was one voice raised on Widman's behalf, that of Peter Miller, who not content with mere words set out at once for Valley Forge, where, aided by General Lee, who in more peaceful times had been a frequent visitor at Ephrata, he secured a prompt audience with Washington.

Brother Jabez, as Miller was known among the brethren, begged long and earnestly for the life of the innkeeper, but the patriot commander refused to interfere, pleading the urgent need for severity in such cases. "Otherwise," he added, "I would cheerfully release your friend." "Friend!" was Miller's astonished reply, "he is my worst enemy, my unwearied reviler. And being such, my creed commands me to pray for those who despitefully use me, and as such, I pray and beseech you in his behalf." Washington could not resist this noble prayer for a bitter enemy. "The pardon is granted," runs the chronicle, "and the prior, with anxious heart lest he should be too late, fares forth on a second errand of mercy. After a weary day's journey he reaches the block-house where Widman is confined. He finds a hollow square drawn up before it, a gibbet in the centre, and the innkeeper, with the rope around his neck, addressing the crowd. Peter Miller pushes his way through the throng and hands his papers to the commanding officer. The culprit sees him and his pale face is covered with blushes. Once more he raises his voice and tries to excuse his conduct, appealing to Peter Miller to forgive him now that he stands on the brink of eternity, but the officer curtly interrupts him with, ' Your life is spared, and here is your deliverer.' " The colonial records show that Widman did not escape all punishment, for his property, consisting of several farms and houses, was confiscated and sold in March, 1780.

The inscription on the stone above Miller's grave in the burial-ground at Ephrata, where the brethren and sisters lie in long rows under the soft green turf, tells the visitor that he " fell asleep September 11th, 1796."

But long before his death the fortunes of the Order of the Solitary began to decline, since with each passing year the world's people trespassed more boldly on the wilderness refuge of the brotherhood. Thus, time came when only a few aged monks and nuns lingered in the desolate convents, and in 1814, with the consent and at the request of the few surviving members, the Seventh-Day Baptists of Ephrata were incorporated to succeed to the property rights of the dying fraternity, since which time the land and buildings of the Solitary have been held in trust for " religious, charitable, and literary objects."

In these latter days Ephrata has become a popular summer resort, but the follower in the footsteps of Beissel, when he alights in the quaint old town, will travel in another direction than that taken by the modern pleasure-seeker. A half-mile walk from the railroad station brings one to an old wooden bridge, spanning the Cocalico, on the farther side of which a footpath, winding to the left past an ancient grist-mill, leads to Bethania and Saron, where once dwelt the monks and nuns of Ephrata. Entering Bethania's low and narrow door,—outside, a high gable roof, small windows, and shingled walls, blackened by time and the elements, give the huge structure a strange and outlandish appearance,—one finds one's self in a dimly lighted hallway running the entire length of the building. No sound breaks the stillness and the place seems wholly deserted. Tiny cells, bare of furnishing, flank both sides of the hallway just referred to, and the upper stories, reached by dark and narrow stairways, are arranged in much the same way. Time was, as I have shown, when Bethania housed many score of solitary brethren, but its only occupants at the present day are a few families of Seventh-Day Baptists.

Saron, or the Sisters' House, stands at the other end of a well-kept meadow. In crossing to it two small buildings are passed, one of which was long occupied by Beissel, the founder of Ephrata and the cloister. Both of these are now fallen into sad decay. Saron, the present home of a number of widows and spinsters, all members of the

Seventh-Day Baptist Church, in outward appearance bears a close resemblance to its mate, Bethania, but its interior has been greatly altered, probably to meet modern needs and demands. In one room, devoted to the purpose, are displayed a number of rare and beautiful manuscripts and a goodly collection of the books printed on the famous press of Ephrata, the specimens of ornamental penmanship shown clearly evidencing the skill and adeptness in this field of comely Anastasia and her pious sisters. After Bethania and Saron the most interesting relic of Beissel's society is Saal, which from Ephrata's infancy until the present time has been used as a place of worship. Charts and allegorical pictures, the latter portraying the life and destiny of the inmates of the cloister, cover the walls of the main room, and above its entrance hangs a tablet on which is inscribed,—

> " The house is entered through this door
>   By peaceful souls that dwell within.
> Those that have come will part no more,
>   For God protects them here from sin,
> Their bliss is found in forms of love,
> That springs from loving God above."

The Order of the Solitary had at least one singular offspring. I have said that that which was most remarkable at Ephrata was the music. About the year 1800 it attracted the attention and evoked the admiration of one Peter Lehman,—and thus the nunnery of Snow Hill had its origin, for when, a little later, he became the pastor of a Seventh-Day Baptist church near Waynesboro, in the southern portion of Franklin County, Pennsylvania, then a comparative wilderness, he at once introduced the Ephrata church music there, and on a farm belonging to one of his followers laid the foundations of a religious institution patterned after the Order of the Solitary. At first there were only four inmates of the Snow Hill nunnery, single men and women, who agreed to become members, to work for their board and clothing, and to abide by the rules of the society. However, others soon joined the original members, and for many years the average number of persons living at the nunnery was fifty. Any Seventh-Day Baptist in good standing was eligible to membership in the " Monastical Society

of Snow Hill" provided he or she was willing to come out from the world and be separate; to give up all worldly goods to the
society and to lead a life of celibacy. The
vows were not necessarily for life, but very
few of those who entered ever returned to
the world. No one having a husband or
wife living was admitted, but widows and
widowers could become members. All new-
comers were obliged to serve a novitiate of
one year, after which, if satisfactory, they
were admitted to full membership and received a new name. Those who desired to
marry or to see more of the world were free
to leave and carry with them everything
they had brought in, but nothing they had
acquired while members of the order.

The brothers at Snow Hill raised stock,
tilled a large farm, and operated a flouring-
mill, while the sisters sowed and spun flax,
wove and made linen and woollen cloth, and
gathered herbs for their own use. The sisters who cooked one week made butter the
next, and the millers of one seven days
tended sheep the following half fortnight.
Idleness was not permitted, neither was over-

work, and an abundance of wholesome food robbed the life of the monastics of severity. The whole society ate their meals in one dining-room, the male members by themselves at one long table and the females at another. Prayers were attended twice a day, at five o'clock in the morning and at sunset, the brothers and sisters again sitting apart from each other. The observance of the Seventh Day began with services on Friday evening, and continued all of Saturday, but, of course, on the First Day, or Sunday, ordinary vocations were pursued. Interspersed with the secular duties at the nunnery were classes in history, music, and theology, to the study of which all applied themselves diligently, under the administration of Peter Lehman, who acted as prior or father. As was to be expected, its music was the most attractive feature of the Snow Hill society, and the singing of its choir, after years of study and practice, is described as exceedingly sweet and beautiful. The evening service of song was held in the small, low-roofed chapel, indented in the walls of which are copies in ancient German text of the Lord's Prayer and other inscriptions, now almost obliterated by the ravages of the years, and travellers often journeyed many miles to listen to it. Nor did the brothers fail to carry on an active and successful propaganda among the people of the countryside. Hundreds of converts were baptized in the brook which runs through the society's farm, and the affiliated members of the order soon spread through the surrounding country, becoming prosperous farmers and artisans, and building for themselves a church on the nunnery farm. Annual meetings are still held in this old building, and to them come from the adjacent country and from Ohio and Kentucky the numerous descendants of the builders, who cling with pious, single-minded zeal to the faith of their forbears.

The home of the Snow Hill devotees was, in most respects, a fitting one, a group of buildings erected at different periods, low and rambling in appearance, with quaint dormer-windows and a belfry of antique pattern surmounting the roof of the main structure, the interior of which consists of a maze of rooms through which it is almost impossible for the stranger to find his way. The original cloister was erected in 1814, the chapel in 1836, a brothers' house in 1839, and a sisters' house four years later. Shops were also erected all over the place, each half a century ago a hive of industry. Now, however, all is changed at Snow Hill. The causes which worked for the decline and fall of the Order of the Solitary have also brought about the eclipse of its offspring. The tokens of ruin and decay are everywhere apparent about the buildings at Snow Hill, and for more than three decades the waning of the fortunes of the society has been rapid and continuous, old age and disease fast filling the graveyard in the meadow, while no new members came to take the places made vacant by death. The last brother and sister died several years ago, and Snow Hill, like Ephrata, now belongs to the past.

CHAPTER XII

BETHLEHEM AND AROUND THERE

TIME has wrought many changes, but the spirit of Zinzendorf still hovers over Bethlehem and Nazareth, and the Moravians of to-day remain faithful to the beautiful creed and the tender and gracious traditions of their fathers. Bethlehem nestles among the hills of Pennsylvania's beautiful Lehigh valley, and its ancient buildings, elbowed by snug modern houses, silently recount a peaceful history, dating back to the time when, threescore years more than a century ago, a small Moravian missionary band took shelter by Lehigh's stream, and founded there, amid forest hills and on land bought from William Penn, a wilderness home.

It was in the early winter of 1740 that the founders of Bethlehem cut down the first trees and built the log hut which sheltered themselves and their animals until the return of spring. Previous to that time a handful of Moravians had settled in Georgia, but when England began war against Spain and demanded that the peace-loving Moravians should perform military service, they concluded to remove to Pennsylvania. Count Zinzendorf, their leader, arrived from Germany before the second house in the new settlement was completed, and celebrated the Christmas Eve of 1741 with his followers. The latter had intended to call their new home Beth Leschem,—house upon the Lehigh,—but towards midnight of the Christmas Eve in question Zinzendorf, deeply moved by the spirit of the occasion, seized a blazing torch, and marching around the room, began singing a German hymn:

"Not from Jerusalem, but from Bethlehem, comes that which benefits my soul."

And thus it was that the infant settlement came to be called Bethlehem. A very remarkable man was the one who gave the town its name. The descendants of the followers of the Protestant reformer and martyr John Huss, the Moravians, driven like

chaff before the wind, for three centuries
endured persecutions as bitter as they were
unrelenting, but with the birth of Zinzendorf
in 1700 the hour of their deliverance struck.
Descended from an ancient and noble Aus-
trian family, Zinzendorf was one of the
truly great men of his time, combining in
signal and rare degree the qualities of the
statesman, the administrator, the poet, the
preacher, and the missionary. Carefully
educated and with a brilliant public career
at his command, when in 1722 a small band
of Moravians, fleeing from Bohemia, found
refuge on his estate at Berthelsdorf, he saw
in their coming the hand of God, and thereafter and until his death was the wise leader
and loving protector of the persecuted sect.
Ordained a bishop of the Moravian Church
in 1737, Zinzendorf proved a marvel of un-
tiring endeavor, travelling constantly and
preaching and writing almost without ces-
sation. His missionary zeal was absorbing
and persistent, and he was never so happy as
when making converts to his faith. Eloquent, resolute, and forceful, he builded better than he knew, and before he died his fol-

lowers had carried their faith to the uttermost parts of the earth.

Nowhere was it planted more firmly than at Bethlehem. The first settlement in Central Pennsylvania, then the freest and most tolerant country in the world, for upward of a hundred years the little town by the Lehigh was an exclusive church settlement, offering a unique example of the union of church and municipal order and authority. No one was permitted to engage in business pursuits or handicrafts within its corporate limits unless he was a member of the Moravian Church; and its secularities were administered by a board of overseers appointed by the congregation council. Still, the colony prospered from the first. Thriving mercantile and manufacturing enterprises were speedily set on foot; the settlement soon contained skilled operatives in almost every trade that could be mentioned, and during the Revolutionary period Bethlehem became one of the most important manufacturing centres on the continent, its shops and factories rendering invaluable aid to the patriot cause.

Moreover, during the first years of its existence the Bethlehem community presented almost a counterpart of the early Christian community of Jerusalem, who "had all things in common." In this missionary economy the products of the labor of the entire community were held in common, for the providing of a livelihood for all, the members carrying on a general housekeeping, in order to secure the necessary support of the men and women chosen to give up all their time to missionary labors among the scattered settlers along the Atlantic coast, and especially among the Indians of Connecticut, New York, and Pennsylvania. Marvellous was the success of the Moravian evangelists among the aborigines. Villages of Christianized and civilized Indians sprang up in the heart of the wilderness, and made it to blossom as the rose with the fruits of industry and peace. Mysterious seems the Providence which permitted these Indian settlements, one by one, to be blotted out in fire and blood at the murderous hands of allied white and red foes; and the tragedies of the two Gnadenhüttens (Tents of Grace)—the one in 1755, on the Mahoning Creek, in Eastern Pennsylvania; the other in 1788, on the Muskingum River, in Northern Ohio—mark pages in earlier American history as dark as they are inscrutable.

The "economy" which the church organization of the Moravians devised for the Bethlehem community lasted only thirty years,—having served its purpose it was discontinued,—but until 1844 the town and its environs remained under the absolute control of the Moravian Church. In the year named the exclusive system was abandoned by vote of the church council,—before that time only those who affirmed allegiance to the Moravian faith could hold property in the town,—and since then great changes have been wrought in Bethlehem. New elements, business and social, have made themselves felt in the town, which has become an active business community, but the Moravian Church, strong in the sustaining power of a heroic and consecrated past, still dominates Bethlehem, and its schools, edifices, and institutions are the most conspicu-

SISTERS' HOUSE, BETHLEHEM, PENNSYLVANIA.

ous objects to be seen in a walk about the city.

Such a walk is pretty sure to lead one past the old Sun Inn, built by the Moravians in 1758, and the shelter in its early days of Washington, Lafayette, and many other famous men; the Moravian Theological College and Female Seminary, the latter the first boarding-school for girls established in the colonies, and the several houses wherein dwelt respectively the members of the different choirs or divisions of the congregation. Thus, the unmarried women lived in what is still known and used as the Sisters' House, —the dwelling of the Single Sisters' Choir. It must not be supposed, however, that these sisters were nuns and recluses, as their name and mode of life might at first suggest. On the contrary, like the members of the Single Brethren's Choir, they simply occupied a common dwelling apart from the other choirs, mingling freely with the rest of the community in daily intercourse. Even this primitive manner of living has now been discontinued, nor are the members of the different choirs longer distinguished by the slight differences in dress, as was customary in bygone years, when the choir to which a woman belonged was known by the color of the ribbon in her cap: the Single Sisters wearing pink, the Married Sisters blue, and the Widows white, while the young members of the Great Girls' Choir had their caps trimmed with red ribbons.

Memory of these neglected customs, however, serves to recall the somewhat rigid regulations in reference to age and sex which in old times governed every Moravian community. There was no courtship, and it was unusual for the bride to have seen her intended husband previous to the betrothal. Both ministers and laymen submitted the decision of their connubial choice to lot, discovering in this now discarded practice proof of a higher order of Christianity, in which all things were submitted to the supreme will and direction. Still, confession must be made that, in cases where the affections were already placed, the decision by lot was often evaded. In such cases the romance of courtship usually led to a suspension from the rights and privileges of the particular congregation where the infringing parties resided. They were asked to remove without its pale, and were no longer considered members.

Adjoining the Sisters' House at Bethlehem and connecting it with the Congregation House—the abode of the ministers and their families—is the old Bell House, now occupied by members of the congregation, but formerly serving for the occupation of the female seminary. On the opposite side of the street is located the Widows' House, still occupied by members of the Widows' Choir; and close to this group of buildings is a little chapel, used even to this day for the holding of German services, and a larger church edifice, with odd open-belfry steeple, which overlooks an ancient cemetery. This Moravian God's Acre is, strange as it may seem, one of the most cheerful spots in Bethlehem. The townspeople find it pleasant to sit in, and in the summer-time women and children spend entire afternoons there. Nearly threescore of the Indian converts to the Moravian faith are buried in this field. One of them is Tschoop, believed to be the father of

Cooper's Uncas. Tschoop was a Mohican chief, famed for his bravery and eloquence. In 1741 Christian Rauch, a Moravian missionary, went to Tschoop's hut and asked him if he did not want to save his soul. " We all want to do that," was the chief's reply. Rauch explained the Christian religion to him, and prayed and pleaded with him even with tears, but apparently in vain. He remained for months near the Indian. Tschoop was a fierce, gigantic savage, the terror of the whites, and Rauch was small in build and mild of temper. The chief at last professed Christianity, and was baptized under the name of John. In a letter which he sent to the Delawares he says, " I have been a heathen. A preacher came to preach to me that there is a God. I said, ' Do I not know that? Go back whence thou camest.' Another came and preached that it was ruin for me to lie and get drunk. I said, ' Do I not know that? Am I a fool?' Then Christian Rauch came into my hut and sat down beside me day after day, and told me of my sins and of Jesus who died to save me from them. I said, ' I will kill you.'

But he said, ' I trust in Jesus.'   So one day,
being weary, he lay down in my hut and fell
asleep.   And I said, ' What kind of man is
this little fellow?   I might kill him, and
throw him into the woods, and no man would
regard it.   Yet there he sleeps, because Jesus
will take care of him.   Who is this Jesus?
I, too, will find the man.' "

Succeeding in his quest, the great chief
preached the Christian religion with the
same fiery eloquence which had given him
power among his people, and for many years
went up and down among the tribes in the
Western wilderness.   The inscription on the
stone above Tschoop's grave says that he
was " one of the first-fruits of the mission
at Shekomo, and a remarkable instance of
the power of divine grace."   Beside the
grave some one has planted a white rose-
bush,—the only one among them all on
which a flower grows.

After Bethlehem the most important Moravian villages in America are Nazareth and
Lititz.   Nazareth is in Northampton County,
Pennsylvania, not far from Bethlehem, and
is one of the quaintest of New World towns.

Perched high among the mountains, its old-fashioned houses, well-shaded streets, and slow-moving people seem to belong to another age. The founding of Nazareth antedated that of Bethlehem. In 1740, Whitefield, the great field preacher, bought the land upon which the town stands, designing to build in the wilderness of Pennsylvania an orphanage for colored children. In the erection of the buildings included in his project Whitefield had recourse to the Moravian craftsmen who had lately fled from Georgia to Pennsylvania. The preacher and his workmen soon quarrelled over religious matters, and the former's funds becoming exhausted about that time, his landed holdings were purchased by Spangenberg, the Moravian bishop and, after Zinzendorf, the most heroic figure in Moravian history. Spangenberg at once took up his residence in the new settlement, which was given the name of Nazareth, and for many years directed its affairs with vigor and wisdom.

The " economy" plan was followed at the outset, and the Nazareth colony prospered

from the first. The " economy of Nazareth"
was dissolved in 1764, and seven years later
the present town of Nazareth was laid out.
In August, 1858, it was incorporated into
a borough, but it is still in every particular
a Moravian village, with characteristics not
to be found in any other town of the United
States. Its most famous institution is Nazareth Hall, a boarding-school for boys.
Erected in 1755, it was originally designed
as a home for Count Zinzendorf, who expected to become a resident of Nazareth, but
the Moravian leader, after his visit in 1741,
never returned to America, and the house
was devoted to other uses. For some years
it was used by Bishop Spangenberg as a
residence, but in October, 1775, was opened
as a boarding-school for boys, and from that
date to this it has been used for educational
purposes, being noted far and wide for the
sound mental and moral training imparted
by its teachers, under whom many of the
makers of Moravian history have begun
their education.

Pleasant and profitable was the life led
by the Nazareth Hall school-boys in the old

days. In the summer season there were swimming excursions, eagerly looked forward to and keenly enjoyed by all the boys. In the autumn there were nutting parties, and in the winter sledding and skating. It was the custom after the first deep fall of snow to go out among the neighboring farmers and engage a convoy of sleighs sufficient for the accommodation of the entire school. The departure was always attended by the music of bells, the cheers of the boys, and the shouts of the spectators, and for a stopping-place some inn was usually selected where the cooking stood in fair repute, and where due notice of the party and of the hour of its arrival had been sent the day before. Another pleasurable custom, now fallen into disuse, was the celebration with feasting and social intercourse of each teacher and pupil's birthday. Then as now life at Nazareth Hall was a charming and happy one, and " no boy," says one who was once a pupil, " ever passed a portion of his youth there without being the wiser and better for it."

Lititz, the third of the Moravian villages

I have named, lies in Lancaster County, and
owes its origin to a vision which in 1742 appeared to George Klein, one of the leaders
of a Lutheran colony which had been established at Warwick, in Lancaster County, not
far from the Dunker village of Ephrata. In
the year just named Count Zinzendorf visited Warwick and preached to its inhabitants.
Klein was the only person in the settlement
who refused to attend the meeting, and was
loud in denunciation of all Lutherans who
were present. That night a vision appeared
to Klein. He saw the Lord face to face,
and received evidence of His displeasure at
the faithful Lutheran's bitterness and denunciation of the Moravian disciple and
missionary. Count Zinzendorf proceeded to
Lancaster from Lititz, where he was to
preach in the court-house. George Klein
was so deeply impressed with the vision
which had appeared to him that he followed
the missionary to Lancaster, heard him
preach, and was there and then converted
to the Moravian faith. He became an ardent and self-sacrificing worker in his new
field. Through him one of the best Mora-

vian preachers and instructors the Bethlehem colony could supply was sent to Warwick, and in 1744 every German settler there had been converted to the Moravian doctrine.

In that year George Klein built the first Moravian place of worship in the settlement, a portion of which still stands in the lower part of Lititz village. In that ancient structure, which was built of logs and called St. James's Church, the Indian missionary, Christian Rauch, began his career as a preacher. In 1754, George Klein gave to the church six hundred acres of land and erected a stone building two stories high for a place of worship. In 1787 the present church was built, but as early as 1760 one of the buildings that stand near the church was erected for a sisters' house, and another quaint structure belonging to the church was built in 1770. These are now included in the famous Moravian Female Seminary of Lititz, known as Linden Hall. It is the oldest young ladies' seminary in the State, its use as a school dating from 1794. The simple but imposing architecture of these old buildings stands in striking contrast to the ornate style of the Memorial Chapel erected in 1883 by George W. Dixon, of Bethlehem, in memory of his daughter Mary, who died soon after graduation at Linden Hall.

In 1756 the name of Lititz was given to the new Moravian settlement, the christening being by Count Zinzendorf himself, and the name that of an ancient town in Bohemia, where, in 1456, the persecuted Moravian Church found refuge. Lititz saw many stirring events during the Revolution. In 1778 it was converted into a temporary hospital for the sick and wounded of the patriot army, and in a field to the east of the town sleep more than a hundred of Washington's soldiers who died of camp fever at that time. However, until 1855, only professors of the Moravian creed were permitted to settle in Lititz, and even at the present time the church is all-powerful in the conduct of its affairs.

One object of peculiar interest which peaceful Lititz holds for the visitor is a solitary grave in the corner of the village cemetery. A large slab covers it entirely, and the inscription tells that he who sleeps beneath it was born in 1803 and died in 1880. Between these two dates runs the long story of an eventful life, for it is the grave of General John A. Sutter, whose mill-race on the bank of the Sacramento was the source of the mighty stream of gold that has flowed from California. Sutter was always a wanderer. Born in Baden in 1803, he graduated from the military school at Berne at the age of twenty, and enlisted in the Swiss Guard of the French army, the successors of that famous band of mercenaries who died so bravely in the marble halls of Versailles thirty years before. After seven years' service he changed his colors and entered the army of Switzerland, in which he served until 1834. Then he put off his uniform, and shortly afterwards came to this country. In 1838, with six companions, he went across the plains to Oregon, and down the Columbia River to Vancouver, whence he sailed to the Sandwich Islands. There he got an interest in a trading vessel, with which he sailed to Sitka and the seal islands towards Behring Strait. Turning southward, after some profitable trading, he arrived at the bay of San Francisco July 2, 1839. The appearance of the country pleased him and he decided to remain.

Sutter made a settlement some distance up the Sacramento River, built a grist-mill, a tannery, and a fort, founded a colony, and called it New Helvetia. He took a commission as captain in the Mexican service, and afterwards served as a magistrate under the same government. He played no active part in the war against this country, and after the annexation he was alcalde, Indian commissioner, and delegate to the constitutional convention of California. In 1848 came the discovery that enriched the world and impoverished him. Marshall, a laborer, digging out the race to Sutter's mill, picked up a rough lump of something yellow, and Sutter said at once that it was gold. The millrace was never finished. The laborer turned his pick in another direction and set to work to dig a fortune for himself. The miller bought a shovel and went to take toll of the yellow sand. The stream that was to turn the mill became suddenly worth more than any grist that it could grind. The sequel is well known. The rushing tide of emigrants overwhelmed the little colony of Helvetia, and wiped out Sutter's imperfect title to his land.

Sutter made a brave fight and a long one. He laid claim to thirty-three square leagues of land, including that on which the cities of Sacramento and Marysville now stand. After long delay the Commissioner of Public Lands allowed the claim, and after more delay the Supreme Court of the United States reversed the decision. Then General Sutter carried his claim before Congress, to go through the tedious experience of most people who take claims there. He was still prosecuting it in 1871, when he happened to come to Lititz to drink the wholesome waters of its spring. The quiet of the place and the peaceful life of its people appealed to the restless old man, who was beginning to get tired of his long battle, and he made his home there "until I get my claim through," he said. He was at Washington still getting his claim through when he died, in 1880, and was brought back to Lititz to be buried, his Moravian neighbors making

room for him in the corner of their cemetery.
Grass grows thick about his resting-place,
while overhead, on sunny summer afternoons, rustle the leaves of the lithesome elm;
and one turns from the quiet spot knowing
that here the time-worn wanderer sleeps
more soundly than ever he did in life, and
that with the dead all is well.

The creed of the Moravians has ever been
a brief and simple one. They accept the
Holy Scripture as the Word of God, the only
authoritative rule of religious faith and practice. " The great theme of our preaching,"
says one of their writers, " is Jesus Christ,
in whom we have the grace of the Son,
the law of the Father, and the communion
of the Holy Ghost. The word of the cross,
which bears testimony to Christ's voluntary
offering of himself to suffer and to die, and
of the rich treasure of divine grace thus
purchased is the beginning, middle, and end
of our preaching."

The Moravians eschew dogmatizing and
avoid controversy. Quiet earnestness and
cheerful piety mark their daily life wherever
found, and even death itself is met by them

with sweet and cheerful resignation. When one of their number dies, the fact is announced by four trumpeters, who mount to the church tower, and, one standing at each corner, facing north, south, east, and west, play a solemn dirge. Immediately after death the body is taken from the home and is placed in the dead-house, which is a small stone building in the rear of the church. There it is kept three days. On the third day the body is brought from the dead-house to the lawn nearby, where the coffin is covered with a white pall, on which is embroidered in blue silk, "Jesus, my Redeemer, Liveth." The dead person is never referred to as being dead, but as having "gone home." After an ordinary funeral service over the coffin the procession starts for the cemetery, which is but a few rods in the rear of the church. The procession moves in the following order: Children lead the line, moving two by two, with their teachers. A brass band, with soft instruments, follows, playing solemn music, which is always that of some hymn expressive of a hope of eternal life and a glorious resurrection. Then come the clergy, the bier, and the relatives, who are followed, if the dead person is a brother in the church, by the brethren, and if a sister, by the sisters of the church. The coffin is lowered in the grave while hymns are sung, and the procession returns in the same order to the church. Here coffee and buns are served, and over this simple repast the friends discuss the good qualities of the departed spirit. The Moravian idea of death is an easy transition from this to the better world, and they only allude after the services to the bright future on the sunny side of the life which has ended only to be renewed in a more beautiful world. Therefore they wear white rather than black at all funerals.

Music, as I have just inferred, plays a leading part in the social and religious life of the Moravians. A love of melody is inherent in them, and in the old days at Bethlehem concerts were regularly given by an orchestra of amateur musicians, aided by the voices of the Sisters' Choir, all of whose members receive a careful vocal training. The most charming of them all was that on the anniversary of Whit-Monday. This entertainment was called the Musical Festival, and lasted the whole day, during which, in addition to a well-selected programme, an oratorio was usually presented. Again, in the Moravian village of Nazareth the citizens were wont in other years to assemble in the evenings and rehearse many of the symphonies of Haydn and other composers. A favorite at these gatherings was the " Farewell," signalized by the successive disappearance of the lights. One performer after another, each as he closed his part, blew out his taper, the music meanwhile growing fainter and falling gradually to a pensive andante, until the last survivor of the gay symphony was left alone, seeming, as the notes of his violin died away and he quenched his own taper, to close the scene and drop the curtain on some fine dramatic act.

The most characteristic of all music among the Moravians is that of the trombone, played mostly in the open air,—on the belfry, in the graveyard, or at the church door. Here the Moravian hymn is drawn out with wonderful expression, and I have never heard music more weirdly beautiful than is evoked from these pensive wind instruments by Moravian players on Easter morning, added reason for this being found, perhaps, in the statement that among this devout people the anniversary of Christ's resurrection is the most reverently cherished, the most impressively observed of all church days.

Let me describe the Moravian celebration of Easter as it is to be witnessed each returning spring in the little village of Salem, North Carolina. Throughout the entire year this queen of the festivals is anticipated with sober pleasure by the elders, and creates visions of happiness in the minds of the young people of the secluded Southern hamlet. Even the observance of Christmas pales before the splendors of a Moravian Easter at old Salem, a fact which may in part be attributed to the balmy weather, which usually favors the Easter period, and helps Moravian maidens to ornament their house of God with the fresh sweet flowers and foliage of the early spring. These floral decorations are artistic in conception and arrangement, and so profuse that the church interior becomes a veritable firmament of evergreens and flowers.

In addition to the products of forest and garden many rare exotics are imported for the occasion or grown within the greenhouses of the town. Festoons of cedar, ivy, and holly hang in ornate curves from oaken rafters, and gracefully converge towards the garnished chandeliers, whose crystal pendants sparkle with the play of every prismatic color. The galleries are embowered, and the tones of the great organ seem almost muffled amid so lavish an orniture of fragrant exotics. The pulpit and the rostrum are also generously decorated; the fresco on the wall behind is concealed by elaborate decorations, and in the centre, deftly fashioned with white hyacinths and roses, shine forth in large letters the words, " Christ is Risen."

The celebration begins on Palm-Sunday, when liturgical services are held, accompanied by a sermon appropriate to the commemoration of Christ's entry into Jerusalem, the exercises presenting a foretaste of the musical feast yet to come. During the Passion Week (between Palm-Sunday and Easter) a number of interesting services are held both morning and evening, and attract a very general attendance. Of these the most solemn and impressive take place on Good-Friday. The following day (Saturday) is called " the Great Sabbath," on which the Love-Feast, in imitation of the apostolical agapæ, is celebrated. This observance is one of the most original and distinctive features of the Moravian Church, and every member of the congregation is present, save the sick and infirm, even the mothers carrying babes being assigned seats in the room adjoining the main auditorium, where prattle and cries may not disturb the services. The specially distinctive feature of this day's worship is the novel service of coffee and sweetened bread. To the air already laden with the scent of flowers is added the delightful aroma of the best Java, distilled in huge urns in the basement below.

At the proper moment as fixed by the programme, the doors facing each aisle on either side of the pulpit are thrown open, and through them file two processions, one of men and one of women, all bearing huge wooden trays containing cakes of sweetened bread. The women, who wear dainty white aprons and snowy mull caps, pass down the right aisle and serve each female member of the congregation with cake; while the men, dressed in conventional black, wait similarly upon their own sex seated on the opposite side of the church. When all are served with sweetened bread, the waiters pass out and return with their trays full of huge porcelain mugs of hot, steaming coffee; these are likewise served the congregation, who, led by the choir, sing through the whole distribution. The choir pauses when the bread and coffee have been passed around; and the minister arises, makes a few remarks, and finally, after asking the blessing of God upon the service, breaks the bread and begins to eat. This is a signal to the congregation to do likewise, after which the choir continues the anthem, which the minister reads out stanza by stanza. The cups and remnants of bread later on are borne out by the same waiters, and after more singing, interspersed by words from the preacher, the congregation rises to receive the benediction, and departs amid sonorous peals from the organ.

To the visitor at Salem during the Easter festivities the early morning services on Sunday in the graveyard are the most solemn and impressive of the entire week. Long before the faint streaks of dawn are seen in the eastern horizon the church band ascends to the belfry in the steeple, high above the roofs of the tallest houses, and there in the deepest darkness that precedes the dawn the sweet, solemn music of a Moravian hymn floats out from the trombones upon the cool, quiet air of early morning,—soft and low at first, each succeeding note swelling in volume, evoking countless echoes that are wafted back from distant vale and hill-side until all the air seems filled with the sweet, joyous strains announcing " Christ is risen."

Soon lights here and there indicate the awakening of the households, increasing in number until no dwelling can be seen with-

out a gleaming casement. All is activity
within each home, and sounds of merry
voices and ripples of youthful laughter are
heard on every side.

Already people are on the streets wending
their way to the church, before whose massive doors the congregation is quickly as-
sembling. The old clock in the steeple peals
forth the hour of five; the pastor comes out
from the church and pauses upon the broad
stone steps beneath the light of a gas-jet.
He reads a litany and a hymn,—which is
sung by the multitude, with whose voices
sound the clear, mellow notes of the cornets.
A procession is formed in twos, and, with
the band at its head playing a sacred hymn,
marches slowly past the church into an avenue lined on either side with majestic cedars
a century old, and then proceeds to the
burial-ground.

Strangely impressive, almost weird, is this
early morning pilgrimage to the city of the
dead. The sombre shadows of the night
are beginning to disappear, as in long line
delicately defined silhouettes wend their
way. At regular intervals, on either side

of the white gravelled walk, sentinel-like,
stand venerable mossy cedars, and the brac-
ing air is sweet with the perfume of the
first flowers of spring. Clearly and slowly
the band plays its measured march, while
echoing footfalls keep perfect time to the
cadence of the plaintive yet joyous melody.
Arriving at the cemetery the band ceases
playing, and with head bared the man of
God reads in slow and solemn tones the
Easter morning litany. Silence, solemn and
profound, broods over the gathered throng,
seeming to stay the breathing of the thousand souls whose faith sheds a radiance of
sanctity and heavenly grandeur upon their
humble and devout expectancy, as on this
balmy morning of the early spring they await,
in spiritual communion with their departed
loved ones, the Resurrection hour. Above
the hill the dawn appears, awaking into life
the sleeping earth, while darkling clouds,
born of the night, flee the presence of coming
day. Then from the voices of the assembled host there bursts a melody of joyous
song, and, mingling with the full, resound-
ing strains of trumpets and trombones, arises

in glad hosannas to the splendent sky, where now shines the sun,—God's symbol of the resurrected life; and earth and heaven peal forth in glad accord, "The Lord is risen! Hallelujah, praise the Lord!"

After this the throng of participants and spectators disperse, but later in the morning, and again in the evening, sermons appropriate to the day are preached, the one delivered at night concluding the formal ceremonies of the Moravian Easter. The music during these services is grander, if possible, than that which accompanies any of the other exercises of Passion Week, and partakes of a more joyous nature.

Though the forms are different the same deeply reverential spirit animates and colors the Moravian celebration of Christmas, which at Bethlehem and in the other Moravian villages of this country on Christmas Eve is solemnly ushered in with a service of song and praise, held in the church appropriately decorated for the occasion, and usually opened with St. Luke's poetic chronicle of the Nativity: "And there were in the same country shepherds abiding in the field

keeping watch over their flocks by night.
And lo! the angel of the Lord came upon
them, and the glory of the Lord shone round
about them: and they were sore afraid.
And the angel said unto them, Fear not;
for, behold, I bring you good tidings of
great joy, which shall be to all people. For
unto you is born this day in the city of
David a Saviour, which is Christ the Lord."

After this simple recital there is a short
discourse and a service of song, followed
by a love-feast, consisting of cakes and
coffee, which are distributed among all present, the congregation and guests often num-
bering at Bethlehem between one and two
thousand souls. During this collation a
portion of Beethoven's mass is performed,
and the German words are sung. Simul-
taneous with the singing large trays of
lighted tapers are brought in and distributed
among the children, this as a prelude to the
most moving feature of and a dramatic close
to the services, for as the singing proceeds
the tapers are extinguished in gradual succession; the mugs are gathered up and carried away; the music wanes slowly into

silence, and the last tones of the organ fall gently upon the ears of the hushed and reverent multitude as its members emerge into the starry December night. Once more a king and Saviour has been born to men!

CHAPTER XIII

THREE GROUPS OF GERMAN MYSTICS

IT is a roundabout journey, though one well worth the making, from Economy by way of Zoar to Amana, the three religio-communistic societies which German mysticism has given to America. Economy, oldest of the three, was founded by George Rapp, a Würtemberg vine-planter, who, despite the depressing surroundings of his earlier years, was in many respects a remarkable personality. Rapp while still a young man became an ardent student of the history of primitive Christianity, and a teacher of much the same doctrines expounded in recent years by Count Leo Tolstoi, save that with the former the speedy second coming of Christ became an absorbing, passionate conviction.

Rapp's followers gradually increased until they numbered three hundred families, simple, credulous souls, who, readily accepting the mysticism of their leader, were given the name of Pietists and made objects of derisive hostility on the part of the regular clergy. In fact, so galling and vexatious did the persecutions to which they were subjected become that they at last decided to seek in America the freedom of conscience and worship denied them in the land of their birth, and to build there a home where they could peacefully await the great change which they believed to be at hand. Six hundred of them, having made the long ocean voyage in safety, purchased five thousand acres of land and built a town at Butler, Pennsylvania, and on February 15, 1805, with Rapp as their leader, formally organized the Harmony Society. Its founders believing that the community of goods practised by the first Christians was not one of the temporary phases of a new religious movement, but rather a fundamental principle intended to endure eternally, made it the basis of their organization; and all, following Rapp's example, threw their possessions into a common stock, and agreed in the future to share all things in common.

The little colony remained in Butler ten years, when, in 1815, it removed to Posey County, Indiana, where it purchased twenty-five thousand acres of land. But before this fresh migration a radical change had taken place in the government of the society. In 1807, as the result of a great religious awakening and the growing conviction that the marriage state did not tend to perfect purity of life and heart, celibacy was made one of the articles of faith and an indispensable requisite to admission to the society. As in the matter of community of goods, so in the new departure Rapp and his son set an example for the others by cheerfully putting away their wives. Husband and wife were not required to live in different houses, but occupied as before the same dwelling with their family, having separate sleeping apartments, the husband's in the upper story and the wife's in the lower, and treating each other as brother and sister in Christ. Both in Butler and Indiana the Harmonists, who, despite their singular creed, were frugal, industrious, and shrewd, Rapp himself being a man of signal foresight and executive ability, prospered greatly, but the malarial climate of Indiana proved fatal to so many of them that in 1825 they returned to Pennsylvania, and, purchasing thirty-five thousand acres of land, built the town of Economy. Here their long wanderings ended, and here, at the source of the Ohio, their scrupulous self-denial and wise division of labor caused their wealth to increase like magic. The silks, blankets, broadcloths, flannels, and whiskey made at Economy—deserted mills and factories show what a hive of industry the town once was—became famous, while their great farms, not a foot of which is even now permitted to lie idle, yielded abundant harvests, the membership of the society increasing in the mean time to over one thousand souls, to every one of whom the word of Father Rapp was law.

But in 1831 dissensions arose which for a time threatened the existence of the society; and the story of their origin and final settlement forms, perhaps, the strangest chapter in the history of Economy. From the first Rapp's policy was one of exclusion, and he sought by every means at his command to prevent intercourse between his followers and the outer world. Members of the society were not allowed to learn English or to have communication with those who spoke it, and could not walk outside the lands of the society unless their business required it. Thus Rapp raised a wall around his followers over which they might not pass, and held them docile and content within the magic enclosure, and to-day the stranger who visits Economy meets native Americans of threescore-and-ten to whom the language of the country, wherein their long lives have been spent, is wholly unknown. Only once did Rapp depart from this policy of exclusion, and then, as I have hinted, the result was disastrous.

In 1820 one Bernard Miller startled the citizens of Frankfort-on-the-Main by claiming that he had received a commission from God to announce the speedy reappearance of His Son; and in circulars spread broadcast over Europe he called upon the devout of life and thought to assemble in one place to await the second coming of the Redeemer, soon gathering about him a small band of enthusiasts, who looked upon him as their leader and gave him the name of Count de Leon. In due time a letter from Miller came to Rapp, in which the writer expressed his conviction that America had been selected as the future home of the chosen of God, where they were to watch for the coming of His Son, and announced his desire, with his adherents, to join the Harmonists at Economy. This they were cordially invited to do, and in the winter of 1831 Miller and forty of his followers, all males, arrived and were received with the highest honors. Rapp, however, soon discovered that he and his people had little in common with the new leader, whose luxurious tastes were in striking contrast with the severe self-denial practised by the Harmonists, and he accordingly ordered Miller and his companions to at once leave Economy.

Afterwards consent was given for them to remain until spring, and this clemency was ungratefully employed by Miller to incite a revolt against the rule of Rapp and the practice of celibacy, succeeding so well that two hundred and fifty Harmonists finally signed a declaration proclaiming him the leader of the society. The great majority, however, remained faithful to Rapp, and peace was in the end secured by a covenant in which the malcontents in consideration of the sum of one hundred thousand dollars agreed to leave Economy and relinquish all claim upon the society. The seceders with the money paid them purchased eight hundred acres of land, and under Miller's leadership founded the New Philadelphia Society at what is now Phillipsburg, Pennsylvania. The rules of the new were identical with those of the old, save in the matter of marriage, but Miller's prodigality soon exhausted its means and credit, and the seceders, convinced of the folly into which he had led them, compelled him to withdraw. Tired of his rôle of religious enthusiast, Miller, with his forty original followers, embarked for the Southwest, filled with visions of conquest even more daring than had animated Aaron Burr a score of years before, but died of cholera at Alexandria, Louisiana.

Rid of the malcontents, the parent society

continued on in the even tenor of its way, with Rapp at its head until his death in 1847 at the age of ninety. From first to last the attitude of the Harmonist chief towards his followers was that of a mild and kindly despot. His word was law, and "Father Rapp says it" sufficed to settle all questions of duty, sacred or secular, and to quiet controversy. The official advisers, provided by the written rules of the society, were uniformly treated as figure-heads at the council-board, and quickly degenerated into useful police for the enforcement of distasteful measures. Never, however, if the enforcement of celibacy is excepted, did Rapp abuse the irresponsible authority he had arrogated to himself. Instead, he exercised it with singular fidelity to the well-being of the society, until the close of what, in the main, was an unselfish and saintly life. Nor did he ever lose faith in the speedy second coming of Christ. Economy's solitary night-watchman was required to call out hourly, as he patrolled his beat, "A day is past, and a step made nearer the end: our time runs away, but the joys of the kingdom will be our reward," while for many years everything was kept in readiness which the society would have needed for the journey to the Holy Land. Even the waxing and waning of the prophetic year of 1836, long singled out for the Redeemer's return in glory to the world, did not shake Rapp's belief in the chiliastic promises, and when the society during the winter of 1845 was blest with a notable religious revival, its venerable chief, discerning in the event a sure prognostic of the longed-for era, buckled himself to the work of preparation for the saintly march to Jerusalem with all the enthusiasm of youth.

Two years later Rapp was laid on his death-bed, and then last of all the Harmonists was the old prophet of the society to recognize his impending end. Taken by surprise, even the cold touch of the angel of death did not break the beatific spell of half a century, and one of the watchers at his bedside through the last night of his life put on record this description of the final scene: " Father Rapp's strong faith in the literal fulfilment of the promises concerning the personal coming of Jesus Christ, and the gathering of the whole of Israel, remained unshaken until the end, as was shown by his last words, for when he felt the grip of the strong hand of approaching death, he said, ' If I did not so fully believe that the Lord has designed me to place our society before His presence in the land of Canaan I would consider this my last.' " Rapp died on the 7th of August, 1847. On the day of his funeral—burials at Economy are severe in their simplicity, the remains of the dead being wrapped only in a winding-sheet and a few words spoken beside the open grave— his followers went from the orchard, where sleep the Harmonist dead, to the town-hall, and decided in the future to have two leaders instead of one. With remarkable unanimity R. L. Baker and Jacob Henrici, who had long been Rapp's most trusted lieutenants, were chosen as his successors. Baker died in 1868, but Henrici remained at the head of the society, hale in body and active in mind, until his death in 1892 at the age of eighty-nine. The senior trustee and present head of the Harmonists is John S. Duss, a young man of forty, who before his admission to the society was a school-teacher at Economy.

The wealth of the Harmonists has been wisely invested and is now enormous. With it the Pittsburg and Lake Erie Railroad was built and controlled by the society until its holdings were sold some years ago at a large increase over the original investment. The society also owns a large portion of the town of Beaver, Pennsylvania, and immense tracts of land in the Dakotas. The prohibition of marriage; the refusal, save at rare intervals, to admit new members, and the gradual thinning of the ranks by death, have decreased the membership of the society, until now less than forty remain. Many of this little band are over eighty, and nearly all of them are verging on threescore years and ten. Until her death a few years ago the one most honored among them was Rapp's granddaughter, Gertrude, a beautiful, white-haired old woman, who in her girlhood was a splendid singer, and who for more than sixty years furnished the music for the Sunday gatherings. Her house remains as she left it, and is a cabinet of things rare and curious, pictures and musical instruments brought from Germany and quaintly blown and painted vases more than a century old.

Life at Economy is puritanical in its regularity and severity. Over four hundred men and women are employed by the society and compelled to give strict observance to its rules, which forbid smoking, whiskey-drinking, and courting within the limits of the town. Males and females live apart and are never permitted to mingle even at work, but so considerate is the treatment they receive that few of them leave except to marry. At five o'clock in the morning every one breakfasts; at six o'clock work commences —the duties of the day being announced by the milkman as he goes his rounds—and continues until ten o'clock, when lunch is served. From twelve to one o'clock is the dinner hour. There is another luncheon at three o'clock and supper at six o'clock. At nine o'clock the bell rings and all must retire. Everything is in common. Grocer, butcher, baker, and milkman visit each house daily, and even the washing is done at the common laundry. Nothing can be bought with money at Economy, and only members of the society handle that article. However, the generosity of the Harmonists is proverbial, and they are kindness itself to the poor people about them. Many orphan children have been reared, educated, and started in life by them, and no unfortunate is ever turned from the town unfed. There is a room at the inn, which, with the store, post-office, town-hall, and church, stands in the centre of the village, especially reserved for tramps, who are kindly cared for overnight, and given a little money when they start on their way in the morning, while other visitors, and curiosity brings many of them, are always sure of a cordial welcome.

No longer able to work, this little band of aged men and women now devote themselves to good works and to those sweet religious meditations which have so long been their consolation and their hope. Twice on every Sunday they gather at the church, with its high-backed, uncushioned pews, and listen to Elder Duss standing in the place of Rapp and Henrici. He speaks briefly and without preparation, but always with eloquence and force. No excuse is accepted for absence from the church, and should one of the members chance to nod during the services, he is called to sit upon the stool of punishment, a solitary bench in the centre of the church, until the meeting is dismissed.

Many of the ancient customs of the fatherland are still observed in Economy. Their Würtemberg ancestors used to celebrate the completion of the annual harvest with feasts and merrymaking, and on the 19th of August of each year the Harmonists observe in fitting manner this beautiful custom of their fathers. Weeks before the day preparations are making for the feast. Wine half a century old is brought from its cobwebbed resting-place, and the choicest calves and beeves are fattened, killed, and roasted. The day's exercises are opened by the playing of the band maintained by the society among its workmen, and at half-past nine o'clock there are services in the church. When all the others have taken their places, the members of the society enter with the trustees and elders at their head. After they are seated there is singing, in which the congregation joins, and a discourse by Elder Duss, followed by more music. Finally, at eleven o'clock, comes the feast. Headed by the band, the society and its employés, with those who are fortunate enough to be guests, march to the town-hall, where the feasting, speech-making, and singing are continued for hours. In the evening they again assemble, and another sumptuous spread, interspersed with music, brings the day to a close.

Besides the harvest-home there are two other great annual feasts at Economy. One of these occurs on the 15th of February, and is designed to fittingly celebrate the foundation of the society in 1805; the other is the celebration of the Lord's Supper in the closing days of October, for the Harmonists partake of the sacrament but once a year, holding that to do so oftener is a violation of the Saviour's wish and will. Music plays an important part in their celebration of the sacrament, as in all their social and religious observances. On the morning of the sacramental day the town is awakened at sunrise by the band playing in the portico of the church. Marching to breakfast still playing, the musicians have no sooner finished their meal than they are on the street again and giving brave attention to their instruments. From house to house they go, arousing the inmates and summoning them to church, where all are required to assemble and listen to a sermon from the head of the society. After the preaching comes the observance of the sacrament. This does not take place in the church, but in the townhall, only members of the society being permitted to communicate or even to be present. There is an elaborate feast prior to receiving the sacred elements, and in the character and preparation of the viands for this repast effort is made to imitate as closely as possible those partaken by Christ and His disciples when they ate the Passover for the last time. Unleavened bread and a large dish of a peculiar kind of soup are placed in the centre of the table, and used by the Harmonists to perform the singular ceremony which they term " dipping the sop." At a given signal all dip into the soup a piece of bread, thus converting it into a sop; this in memory of the Saviour's words when asked who should betray Him,—" He that dippeth his hand with me in the dish, the same shall betray me." Dipping the sop is performed with the utmost solemnity by the Harmonists, who regard it as an humble confession that they have betrayed Christ many times by their sins against Him. After this ceremony the bread is broken and the cup prepared by Elder Duss, who blesses both, and all partake in silence. Then, one by one, they pass from the hall, and the celebration of the sacrament is finished.

What with its quiet, grass-grown streets, its weather-beaten, many-gabled houses, and its carefully tended gardens, Economy has been termed by an acute observer " a fine Rhenish village left behind intact from the eighteenth century." One is tempted to apply the same description to Zoar, the home of the Separatists, fourscore miles to the west of the Economy; nor is the resemblance an accidental one, for the Separatists came from the same part of Germany as the Harmonists, and like them suffered voluntary

exile for their religious belief. The founders of both communities belonged to the
working class, Rapp, the head of the Harmonists, being a vine-planter, and Joseph
Baumeler, the leader of the Separatists, a
weaver. The latter was endowed, however,
with an original and inquiring mind and
exceptional earnestness of purpose. While
still a young man he became an ardent student of the writings of Boehme and other
mystics, finally extracting from them a new
religious creed, not unlike that framed by
Rapp a few years before. Like Rapp also,
Baumeler proved a zealous propagandist,
and those who shared his belief, drawn
mainly from the peasant class, soon numbered several hundred.

Nor did they escape the bitter persecution
which had formerly been the lot of the Harmonists. For some ten years they bore the
burdens of flogging, fines, and imprisonment
in uncomplaining silence. Then their sufferings attracted the attention of a number
of wealthy English Quakers, who, in 1817,
furnished money to pay their passage to the
United States, at the same time contributing

a handsome additional sum to assist them
after their arrival. The Zoarites, to the
number of two hundred men, women, and
children, landed at Philadelphia in August
of the year named. Aided by their Quaker
friends, they at once purchased several thousand acres of land in the Tuscarawas valley
in Ohio and laid the foundations of the town
of Zoar, the remaining members of the sect
joining them in the spring of 1818. At first
an essay in communism was not thought of,
but it soon became clear that success could
only be achieved by associated effort, and
two years after the arrival at Zoar articles
of agreement for a community of goods were
executed and signed, each signer throwing
his belongings into the common lot, and
vowing to do the same with any property of
which he might thereafter become possessed,
while at the same time Baumeler was formally installed as the spiritual and temporal
head of the society.

Frugal and industrious, the Separatists
from the first prospered under the communal
system. Nearly every handicraft was represented among the original members of the

society, and the various shops erected at once attracted the patronage of the farmers of the countryside and became a source of profit. This, with their careful farming and successful cattle-raising, enabled them in a few years to pay for their lands and erect roomy and comfortable buildings. They own at the present time seven thousand acres of land, covered in part by orchards and vineyards, besides thousands of head of the finest cattle and sheep. Zoar has also its tin, tailor, and shoe shops, its own saddlery, brewery, carpenter and cabinet shops, and its own woollen-, flour-, planing-, and saw-mills. One of the most interesting places to visit is the cow barn at milking-time. The society keeps about one hundred cows, which are driven to pasture in the morning, and at sunset may be seen ambling contentedly homeward to the musical clink of many-toned cow-bells. Upon reaching the large barn the herd separates, each division entering its own door, and each cow finding and occupying her own stall and knowing her own name. The young girls then come out in numbers, and to each is deputed the milking of three or four cows. The little children sometimes bring tin cups, and each receives as much milk as he or she can drink.

Life at Zoar is very plain and simple. Each dwelling-house accommodates several families, but each family lives alone. A member is allowed a certain number of gowns or suits per year, and groceries and provisions of all sorts are obtained in the same way, an ample allowance for each family being dealt out on application. Some of the girls and older women earn a small amount of money by knitting thread laces, which they sell to visitors at the hotel, erected some years ago by the society for the reception of summer guests, and thus secure a little spending money of their own, but with this exception no member handles money, all profits from the harvests and workshops being deposited in the society treasury. In the long days of summer every one arises at daylight and labors until six o'clock at night, the women at seed-time and harvest working beside the men in the field. In the winter season work is continued in the shops and factories until eight o'clock in the evening, these long hours, however, being lightened by breakfast, dinner, and supper, and a morning and afternoon lunch. On summer nights the men practise in the village band, or smoke and quaff their beer in a tiny public garden filled with masses of blooming flowers and clumps of well-trimmed shrubs, while the women visit from one vine-covered cottage to another, and the children play upon the common in front of the church. On Sunday there are three religious services. At the morning service one of Baumeler's discourses—he died at a ripe old age after having directed the affairs of the society for a quarter of a century—is read by one of the older members; the afternoon meeting is devoted to the children, and the evening gathering to song and praise. No services are held during the week.

The history of the Separatists, similar in other respects, offers a marked contrast to that of the Harmonists in the matter of celibacy, for while the older society accepted it only as a second thought, the Separatists at first made it one of the conditions of membership, only to give it up in after-years. Celibacy was one of the fundamental doctrines of Baumeler's curious creed. He believed that God created Adam both a male and female, or, as he expressed it, "Adam was a masculine maiden possessing both the male and female elements of generation." The separation of the female element from Adam by the creation of Eve he regarded as the result of some sin on Adam's part, and for that reason he warmly condemned the marital state as impure and unholy. But with all his mysticism Baumeler was refreshingly practical, and when in 1832 cholera decimated the ranks of the Separatists and threatened their society with extinction, he gave his followers permission to marry, and himself set the example by taking a wife. Of the children since born and reared within the confines of the society, about one-half have remained faithful to the creed and customs of their fathers. Still, the Separatist Society now has but one hundred and ten active members, and this number is said to be annually decreasing, for the railway when it came to Zoar a dozen years or more ago brought the spirit of unrest in its train, and with the broader vista thus opened before them many of the villagers have tired of the whilom monotony of their lives and sought individual preferment in other fields. As a result the community of the Separatists is steadily dwindling away, and in a few years at most their peaceful haven will have become a part of the greater world about it.

But if the days of Economy and Zoar are numbered, the Society of the Inspirationists at Amana, Iowa, appears, on the other hand, to still have before it many years of prosperity and growing membership. The Amana community owns some forty thousand acres of rich bottom-lands along the Iowa River, a short hour's ride by rail from Cedar Rapids, and its picturesque villages— there are seven of them—crown the low slopes at two or three miles' distance from each other. These groups of houses are of wood and unpainted, the Amana people claiming that it is cheaper to re-side a house occasionally than to paint it, and the gray-black walls, with their display of vines, set down in quaint geometrical gardens, have a charm as distinctive and restful as it is difficult to describe.

Each village of the Inspirationists suggests a bit of the fatherland transplanted in bulk to the Middle West, and with reason, for the sect sprang from a little band of people who, some eighty-odd years ago, used to gather at the house of Christian Metz, a carpenter of Strasburg. Converts to the mystical teachings of Boehme and Kock, they called themselves Inspirationists, and professed to hold direct and personal communication with God, who, they avowed, made chosen ones among their number His mouth-piece when He desired to speak to His children. Christian Metz was one of these inspired instruments; another was Barbara Heinemann, in many respects the most remarkable person ever connected with the society, and it was due mainly to their influence that the Inspirationists formed their first settlement in America in 1843. Metz and three other members of the society, sent over to select a situation, bought several thousand acres of land near Buffalo, New

York, calling their first village Eben-Ezer, this with reference, doubtless, to the stone set up by Samuel as a memorial of divine assistance. In due time two other villages, called Upper and Lower Eben-Ezer, were laid out, and the end of a decade saw more than one thousand Inspirationists prosperously settled in their new abiding-place. Community of goods was not thought of at first, but the difficulty the craftsmen among the Inspirationists experienced in finding employment in a newly-settled country, combined with other causes, soon made it evident that only by associated effort could the best results be obtained, and so, about 1847, they were "commanded" to hold all things in common and labor together for the common good. Five years later came another "inspired command" for them to move westward,—more land was needed by the community but could not be had at a reasonable price near Buffalo,—and, in obedience to the dictates of the Spirit, the site for a new home was purchased in Iowa. That was in the summer of 1855, and before winter came the first village had been laid out and built.

In choosing a name for it the colonists again went to the Bible and selected Amana, the name of the hill described by Solomon; nor, as other villages were built, did they depart from the original name, but instead devised constant variations of it, as Old Amana, High Amana, South, North, East, West, and Middle Amana.

The wise policy, begun at Eben-Ezer and continued at Amana, of dividing the colony into separate villages has had much to do with the success of the society, which now numbers about eighteen hundred members. It contributes to the quiet and simplicity sought after by the Inspirationists, and at the same time lends greater variety to the communal life than would be the case were there but a single large settlement. The distance from the most easterly to the most westerly village is six miles, but excellent roads and telephone lines render communication easy. The young people in winter skate from one hamlet to another on the canal, dug to carry water to the several villages and protect them from the danger of drought, or walk across the fields in summer. When there is harvesting to be done, the great creaking wagons of a pattern peculiar to Amana carry their loads of workers, of all ages and both sexes, out in the morning and back at night, zest being always given to the day's labors by the possibility of working in the next field to the force from some other village, and the chance of the mid-day luncheon being taken under the trees together.

Farming is, of course, the chief industry of the Inspirationists, but—and herein lies another secret of their success—they also conduct woollen-mills, grist-mills, calico print-mills, hominy-mills, soap-factories, and book-binderies, while each village has its own saw-mill, machine-shop, and store. They own many thousand head of sheep, but as they make three thousand or four thousand yards of woollen goods daily, they buy raw wool in large quantities. They also have their own chemists, doctors, and schools, the last named meriting a passing paragraph.

As soon as a child born in the community is five years old he or she is sent to school.

In the summer seven o'clock is the hour for being on hand, and this is changed to eight o'clock in winter. Until mid-day the little folk sit there on their hard benches going over their lessons, and now and then going over the benches instead when they happen to fall asleep. The boys sit on one side of the room and the girls on the other, the former round and rosy and very tight as to their little German trousers; the latter also round and rosy and looking exceeding quaint in the black crocheted hoods which they seem never to take off. After dinner they all go to school again, but this time to an industrial one, where they are set to work knitting the thumbs of the great Amana mittens, which are famed through all the country round. When the small girls reach the age of seven or eight years they are advanced to the main body, so to speak, of the mitten, the boys being meanwhile put through an apprenticeship at various trades. German is the language of the colony and the one used in the schools, although English is taught in the higher classes. Here again the managers have shown their sagacity if not their loyalty to their native country, for the use of a language other than that of the people about them is clearly a strong tie among the members.

At the head of " The Community of True Inspiration," as the society is officially known, and exercising supervision over its affairs is a board of thirteen trustees, chosen once a year by ballot. Control of the spiritual and temporal affairs of each village is vested in a board of elders, whose members, selected with great care by the central board of trustees, meet every morning to confer together, select the foremen for the different industries, and assign the tasks of the individual members, effort always being made to give the laborer the employment that will be most congenial to him. Record of the affairs of each village is kept by a system of accounting which, although elaborate, is a model of clearness and accuracy, showing at a glance what the village has produced and consumed, what it has sold to other villages or to outsiders, what it has bought, and just what its profits or losses have been. The general accounts of the colony are balanced once a year, when the profits and losses of the whole society are equalized. It should be added, however, that no village bears alone the losses it may have sustained, these being shared by the whole body.

The Inspirationists never handle money save in their dealings with outsiders. Once a year the elders grant each family or adult member of the society credit corresponding to their wants at the village store, against which they are permitted to make purchases. If a member does not spend all of his or her annual allowance, the balance is added to the next year's credit or can be given away. Each village has its own laundry, bakery, butcher-shop, and butter and cheese factory, and wagons from these places make their daily round as they do in cities. Meals are taken in what are called " the kitchens," where the males and females eat at separate tables. There are sixteen of these in Amana proper, with its five hundred and fifty inhabitants, and the food furnished at the five daily meals is good and abundant. Each family has its own house, with a plot of ground around it, and the satisfaction of

the members with their state of life is indicated by the fact that, although all that
can be made from this ground may be retained as private income, it is devoted in
almost every instance to the culture of
flowers. Indeed, the quiet, regular, peaceful life of comfort and plenty led at Amana
has so strong an attraction for the young
people raised there that few leave when they
reach maturity, and those who do so, as a
rule, return in a short time. New members,
however, are admitted with the greatest care,
and only after a long and searching novitiate, the managers wisely preferring to build
slowly but surely out of the material which
they can themselves mould and temper and
adjust.

Besides the doctrine of " direct inspiration" already referred to, the tenets of the
Inspirationist creed include justification by
faith, the resurrection of the dead, and final
judgment. Meetings are held several times
a week, the services usually consisting of
prayer, singing, readings from the Bible, and
brief exhortations. Christmas, New Year's,
and Easter are observed as seasons of special

solemnity, and once a year there is careful examination into the spiritual condition of all the members. Such are the Inspirationists of Amana. In their daily life sober, temperate, and without envy; in their dealings with their fellows kindly, charitable, and just; in their morals singularly pure and blameless, and in intelligence above the average, who would deny them all the contentment and happiness that are theirs?

CHAPTER XIV

IT is an easy pilgrimage, and one well worth the making, from the city which bears his name to the three places which above all others are associated with the life and presence of Washington,—Fredericksburg, scene of his youthful exploits and burial-place of his mother; Mount Vernon, his residence in maturer years; and quiet grass-grown Alexandria, which knew him as burgher, citizen, and neighbor.

Fredericksburg, which borrowed its name from one of the sons of George I., has now become doubly historic from the great battle fought there in December, 1862, but its charm for the visitor still abides in its cherished relics of Washington and his mother. These include the old house within the corporate limits of the town in which both lived and in which she died; the tomb above her grave; the site, on the farther shore of the

Rappahannock, of the house in which he
first lived after his removal from his native
Westmoreland, and the fields about wherein
were enacted the boyish exploits recorded
in the praiseful but not always veracious
chronicles of Parson Weems.

Both of Washington's grandfathers came
from England in 1657 and made new homes
in the same section of Virginia. Augustine,
first of the Washingtons born in America,
chose for his second wife—by his first he
had two sons, Lawrence and Augustine—
Mary Ball, a girl of fortune and excellent
birth, who became, in due time, the mother
of George Washington, the first of a family
of six children. When George was five
years old his father removed from Westmoreland to a plantation which he owned
on the bank of the Rappahannock, opposite
Fredericksburg. The house in which Washington lived with his parents was torn down
threescore years ago, and its site, on the top
of a hill, perhaps a hundred yards from the
river, is now covered by a frame cottage of
modest size. Directly below lies the ferry
where Washington when he was ten years

old, according to Weems,—although this, like many another of the parson's stories, must be taken with a grain of allowance,—threw a stone across the Rappahannock. Fredericksburg folk, it may be added, scout the tale, and even at the present time, with the river sadly shrunken from its former width and depth, the feat described by Weems would be a difficult one for a man of mature years and strength.

Augustine Washington died in 1743, and his widow remained faithful to his memory until her death, nearly fifty years later. Moreover, she reared her children wisely, and one by one saw them prosperously settled in life. With the coming of the Revolution and when he was about to set out for the Continental Congress in Philadelphia, Washington, with loving regard for the comfort and safety of the aging woman, induced his mother to leave her country home and remove to Fredericksburg, nor did he rest content until he had seen her settled in her new quarters. The house Mary Washington selected as her home still stands in Charles Street, but not in its original form.

One end has been altered and the roof raised to give a full second story, changes which have nearly destroyed its former quaintness of aspect.

Fredericksburg saw nothing of Washington during the seven critical, troubled years that followed Lexington and Bunker Hill, but when, shortly after the surrender of Cornwallis at Yorktown, the patriot captain, attended by an imposing suite of French and American officers, started upon what quickly became a triumphal progress to Philadelphia, he stopped on the way to visit the mother who awaited his coming with serene and quiet joy. The meeting took place on the 11th of November, 1781. Washington, "in the midst of his numerous and brilliant suite," I quote from the quaint account of the event given by George Washington Parke Custis, "sent to apprise his mother of his arrival, and to know when it would be her pleasure to receive him. Alone and on foot the general-in-chief of the combined armies of France and America, the deliverer of his country, the hero of the hour, repaired to pay his humble tribute of duty to her whom he venerated as the author of his being." The first warm embrace of greeting over, she drew slowly back, and looking with loving earnestness into his face, said, very softly, " You are growing old, George; care and toil have been making marks in your face since I saw you last."

She, too, had grown old in the intervening years, but when she appeared that night at the ball given by the citizens of Fredericksburg in honor of the victors, leaning on the arm of her son, her noble bearing and the quiet dignity with which she received the addresses of those who came to do her honor prompted Lafayette to remark that he had seen the only Roman matron who was living in his day.

Memory of another meeting between Washington and his mother, last and tenderest of all, comes to mind as one stands before the quiet house in Charles Street. It was in April, 1789, that he came to bid her farewell before leaving for New York to enter upon his duties as first President of the Republic. He found her weak and worn in body and already stricken with the hand of death. When he told her that as soon as his public duties would permit he should return to her, she gently interrupted him, saying that they should meet no more, but that he must go to fill the high place destiny had assigned him. And so they parted, the strong man sobbing like a child as he left her presence for the last time. Four months later she had ceased to live. Washington was at dinner with Baron Steuben and other friends when word came to him that his mother was dead. " My uncle," writes his nephew, who was present, " immediately retired to his room, and remained there for some time alone."

It is a pleasant ride from Fredericksburg to Mount Vernon and takes one along winding country roads often traversed by Washington. In 1741 his half-brother Lawrence served with Admiral Vernon in the disastrous campaign against Carthagena in South America. The following year he returned to Virginia, and was about to sail for England to enter the regular navy when beautiful Anne Fairfax captured his affections, and the spirit of war yielded to the gentler argument of love. They were married in the midsummer of 1748. The death of the elder Washington a few months before had made the young husband owner and master of an estate extending for miles down the Potomac below Alexandria, and Lawrence Washington built for his bride a plain but substantial mansion on the most commanding river outlook, giving it the name of Mount Vernon, in honor of the admiral with whom he had served in the West Indies.

A swift fever made an end of Lawrence Washington in 1752, and his estate passed to his daughter. She soon followed her father to the grave, and by the terms of the original bequest young George Washington, who from the first had been a frequent and much-loved visitor at the mansion, became the master of Mount Vernon and its wide-reaching acres. From his father he had already inherited large landed holdings on the Rappahannock; his new acquisition made him one of the wealthiest planters of the Old Dominion. Coincident with his taking possession of Mount Vernon he began his labors in the service of the colony, first as a surveyor exploring and laying down the bounds of great estates, and then in the military service for the extension of colonial authority and British empire on the Ohio. In the five or six years which followed he rose to a high place on the roll of sagacious military commanders, and the fame of his martial exploits reached the uttermost limits of the colonies.

Frequent absences, however, did not prevent Washington from exercising close and prudent watch over the affairs of his estate, or from prosecuting those affairs of the heart which lend a piquant interest to his career, for the young master of Mount Vernon, like most strong men, was all his life a lover of women, and before he was eighteen had already suffered the pangs of unrequited love. He speaks in letters written at this time of his passion for the " Lowland Beauty," and to the same period may also be assigned two love poems, one an acrostic to " Frances," no doubt some fair maid of Alexandria, and the other a sonnet, interesting only because it shows the depressed state of mind into which its author was thrown by his affairs of the heart. When he was nineteen he courted and was refused by pretty Betsy Fauntleroy, and a little later there grew up in his heart the master passion of his life,—his love for Sally Cary, wife of his friend George William Fairfax and sister-in-law of his half-brother, Lawrence Washington. Sally Cary was already married when Washington first met her, yet this did not prevent him from cherishing a regard for her that for a time threatened to assume "sovereign control" of his ardent nature. His letters are proof that the love he had felt for other amiable women was as water unto wine beside this hopeless attachment for his beautiful neighbor, but fortunately, thanks to time, to the lady's subsequent absence in England with her husband, and, above all, because, Washington being a man of honor and resolute will, the feeling was gradually subdued by him, and his marriage with Mrs. Custis happily ended the episode.

It was in April, 1759, three months after her marriage to Washington, that Martha Custis became the mistress of Mount Vernon. Daughter of Colonel John Dandridge, a belle of the colonial court at fifteen, wife of Colonel Daniel Parke Custis at seventeen, and a widow with two children at twenty-four, Washington met her for the first time while on a military errand to the old Scotch governor, Dinwiddie, at the colonial capital. Their marriage gave him absolute control of one-third of the Custis patrimony, one of the largest fortunes in America. The remainder of the estate came into his hands as guardian.

Washington at this time was in the early flush of his magnificent physical manhood. Straight as an Indian, with limbs cast almost in a giant's mould, his self-contained countenance, agreeable speech, and dignified bearing made his personality most impressive. Probably half of his time at home was spent in the saddle, and this active out-of-door life gave him a glow of health and sense of vigor. Never more at home than on horseback, fox-hunting was his favorite sport, and in his diary for January and February, 1768, it is recorded that he followed the hounds sixteen days and shot on five. Now and then his boldness brought him to grief, but these mischances failed to deter him. At fifty-five he wrote that he was still fond of the chase, which he occasionally indulged in until near his death.

For fifteen years George and Martha Washington enjoyed life at Mount Vernon, he serving in the House of Burgesses and managing his vast estates, she taking complete charge of the domestic economy of the household, and both joining in the exercise of a hospitality as gracious as it was open-handed, unceasing and lavish. The master of Mount Vernon played a forceful part in the events which led up to the Congress of 1774 and finally to the war for independence; and in those trying times his wife supported him with words of approbation and encouragement, writing to a relative, " My mind is made up. My heart is in the cause. George is right. He is always right."

The second Continental Congress met, and Washington was a delegate. Lexington and Concord had fired the heart of the colonies, and the Continental army was organized in June, 1775, with Washington as its commander-in-chief. He wrote to his wife at

Mount Vernon giving directions about the management of his estate, enclosed his will, which " he hoped would be satisfactory," and at once set out from Philadelphia to take command of the Continental forces at Boston. Mount Vernon saw him only twice during the following eight years, and then in the line of military duty, but each winter Mrs. Washington joined her husband at head-quarters to assist in raising the heavy spirits of officers and men and to minister to the sick and suffering.

It was in September, 1781, that Washington suddenly arrived at Mount Vernon, his first visit since 1775, on his way to take command of the forces at Yorktown. But a single night was his stay, and he moved on to close the war in the South and to put an end to the last hope of Great Britain's recovery of her lost colonies. Cornwallis having surrendered at Yorktown, Washington spent a week at Mount Vernon, and then, accompanied by his wife, left for the North to resume command of the army in the vicinity of New York, to put the finishing touches to the war and to give Congress the benefit of his counsel. In November, 1783, Mrs. Washington returned to Mount Vernon, after an absence of two years. The British hauled down the royal standard of King George and evacuated New York. Washington having taken leave of his sorrowing veterans, repaired to Annapolis, where Mrs. Washington joined him to witness the most heroic act of his noble career, —the return of his commission and a conquered nationality to Congress. The same day, December 23, as plain Mr. and Mrs. Washington, they left for Mount Vernon, where they arrived amid the greatest joy of the neighbors on the Christmas Eve of 1783.

The world-wide fame of Washington now made Mount Vernon the shrine of the great men of America and of visiting foreigners of rank and renown. The original mansion quickly proved too small to accommodate the throng of visitors and guests, and in 1785 it was enlarged by the addition of two wings, composing the banquet-hall and the library and the piazza overlooking the river. The detached structures for the farm and domestic offices, the lawn, arboretum, conservatories, and flower- and kitchen-gardens were also constructed or laid out, giving the mansion and immediate surroundings their present appearance.

Of the Fairfaxes, Washington's constant comrades in other days, only Bryan was now left in America, and that good man was getting on in years and making up his mind to take priestly orders. Of Washington's other neighbors, the most important one still living within easy reach of Mount Vernon was George Mason, of Gunston Hall, a patriot of the finest type, the author of that noble paper " The Virginia Bill of Rights," and who in the intervals of useful labor in the Continental Congress returned to his home on the Potomac. To this old manor-house of the Masons, built in 1739 and still standing, although no longer in the possession of the descendants of its first owners, the Washington family was wont at this period to resort for tea-drinking and dinner, visits certain to be returned in kind before the month was out.

Agriculture, after soldiering, was always

Washington's chief delight. To its pursuit he now returned with zest whetted by years of absence from home, and good reason had Brissot de Warville, the French traveller and author, who became chief of the Girondists and died by the guillotine in 1793, to cry out in astonishment at the general's success in farming, when, during his visit to America, he went the rounds of Mount Vernon in the autumn of 1788. The estates were then at the highest pitch of improvement they ever attained, crops of wheat, tobacco, corn, barley, and buckwheat " burdening the ground." What excited the Frenchman's chief surprise was that every barn and cabin, grove and clearing, field and orchard, passed daily beneath the watchful eye of the master. All the busy life of the negro world was regulated by his personal directions to overseers and bailiff. No item was too insignificant to bring before his notice, and the minutest contract for work agreed upon was put into writing. How odd, for example, the agreement with Philip Baxter, the gardener, found, duly signed and witnessed, among Washington's

papers, wherein Philip binds himself to keep
sober for a year, and to fulfil his duties on
the place, if allowed four dollars at Christmas, with which to be drunk four days and
four nights; two dollars at Easter, to effect
the same purpose; two dollars at Whitsuntide, to be drunk for two days; a dram in
the morning, and a drink of grog at dinner,
at noon.''

In barnyards, kennels, and stables there
is continual interest on the part of their master. He makes experiments in breeding
mules with the jacks sent him by the King
of Spain, and thanks Gouverneur Morris for
a couple of Chinese pigs, forwarded from
Morrisania, along with a pair of Chinese
geese. Washington's care of horses is too
well known to need mention here, but one
ceremony of his daily round of his farms,
a ceremony, in season, never omitted by the
general, deserves to be recalled. It was to
lean over the fence around the field wherein
a tall old sorrel horse, with white face and
legs, was grazing luxuriously in the richest
grass and clover Mount Vernon could afford. At the sight of him the old steed

would prick up his ears and run neighing to arch his neck beneath his master's hand. This was Nelson, the war-horse upon whose back, at Yorktown, Washington had received the surrender of Cornwallis. The war ended, Nelson's work was over. Turned out to graze in summer, in winter carefully groomed and stabled, he lived to a good old age, but by his master's strict command was never again allowed to feel the burden of a saddle.

Thus three years passed in quiet and retirement. But they were neither years of leisure nor of rest. The cares of state were thrust upon the privacy of the home life at Mount Vernon. Washington held the leading-strings of the infant republic. The weakness of the Articles of Confederation were apparent to him, and it was in his constant thought to devise some form of strong centralized national governmental authority and administration. He was in communication with the patriots in all parts of the States, hanging together and defaulting in their duty and obligations under the free and easy system of 1777, and it was on the ve-

randa or in the library of Mount Vernon that the preliminary steps were arranged which led to the overthrow of the system of the Confederation and the substitution of the national system in 1787.

It was on a sunny day in April, 1789, that Charles Thomson, secretary of the Continental Congress, arrived at Mount Vernon with the official notification of Washington's election to the Presidency. Reluctant to leave the congenial pursuits and surroundings of Mount Vernon, he nevertheless responded once more to his country's call, and on April 16, 1789, left for New York, the journey being one constant succession of ovations. He inaugurated the new government, and soon after was followed by Mrs. Washington, who established the social institutions decided upon for the executive office and surroundings. During the years of his Presidency Washington occasionally visited Mount Vernon, passing a short time there during the adjournments of Congress. He also took an active part in the establishment of the site and laying the foundations of the capital, which bears his name and lies

almost in sight of his beloved Mount Vernon.

Washington's second term as President
closed in March, 1797, and he at once returned to Mount Vernon. He was now
sixty-five years of age, laden with honors,
surrounded by the confidence of his fellow-
citizens, and in the possession of perfect
health. The care of his estate gave him his
greatest pleasure during his remaining years,
but his regard for the public weal never
weakened, and here and there in the diaries
and private correspondence of the period one
finds proofs of this, which afford at the same
time intimate glimpses of the personality of
the masterful man whose career was now
near its close. Let one of these find a place
in this chronicle. After Adams had been
chosen President, and the outcry against the
Alien and Sedition laws became so loud as
to arouse Washington's apprehension that
the Republicans might carry the country to
the other extreme and the work of disintegration be commenced, he sent a message to
Richmond with a note to John Marshall,
afterwards chief-justice, saying he wished

him to come to Mount Vernon for a week's visit. Marshall, who was an ardent Federalist, got ready, and in a few days reached Mount Vernon, where he was received with great cordiality.

After dinner, when all the other company had retired to the sitting-room, Washington detained Marshall, and soon told him why he had sent for him. "I am uneasy, Major Marshall," said he, "at the rapid growth of these democratic societies and alarmed at the tendency towards the disintegration of our present system. The press is attacking all who wish to maintain the Federal government in its integrity and strength with great violence, and I fear the result of the approaching elections. We need our strongest and most patriotic men in Congress, and I want you to return to Richmond and announce yourself as a candidate."

Marshall made answer that it was impossible; that he was a poor man, dependent upon his practice at the bar, and that the pecuniary sacrifice would be more than he could bear in his present straitened circumstances. Washington argued with him, and

soon got wrought into a violent passion.
No patriot, he declared, would refuse to
serve his country in such an emergency; he
had been making personal sacrifices for the
public all his life, and no one deserving the
name of a man would refuse such a call.

Marshall, in describing the occurrence,
said he had never received such a torrent
of abuse in his life. He thought at one
time Washington would jump on him from
across the table. He retired that night, but
could not sleep. The insults given him
seemed to blister his brain. After rolling
and tossing for a time, he concluded he
would get up early in the morning, slip out,
get his horse, and start home before breakfast. Morning at last came, and as soon as
he could see well he dressed. Fearing to
awake Washington, he took his boots in his
hand and started down the stairway in his
stocking feet; but to his horror he met
Washington in the hall.

" Where are you going, Major Marshall?"
asked the old general.

" I was going out, sir."

" It is too early for you to rise, sir. Return to your room, and I will have you called when breakfast is ready."

Marshall returned to his room, as he said, "to await further orders."

At breakfast Washington was very polite to him. Afterwards he informed Marshall that the horses were ready and that they would ride over the plantation. They rode, returning at three o'clock to dinner. No allusion was made to the row of the previous night. The result of it all was that Marshall stayed the week out, returned to Richmond, ran for Congress, was elected, and took every post that the general wanted him to take. Yet Washington's biographers merely tell us that Marshall was "persuaded by him to enter Congress!"

Once only did Washington leave Mount Vernon after the close of his second term as President. The French monarchy had been overthrown and the Directory were startling the world with horrors. Because the American government would not sanction their butcheries and help shield them from the accumulated vengeance of mankind they warred upon our commerce, imprisoned our citizens, and insulted our commissioners. War seemed inevitable, and Washington was again summoned from his resting-place to resume his arms and defend his country. It must have been a sight to see the old lion once more summoning his brindled sons to battle. His old veterans rallied around him at the sound of his voice, ready to follow their general, to repeat their old hardships, and brave their old dangers. But war was averted, and Washington retired to Mount Vernon—to die.

Two years later his brave wife followed him to the grave. After her death the Mount Vernon estate passed to Bushrod Washington, a nephew of the general. In 1829 it became the property of John Augustine Washington, a nephew of Bushrod. In 1832, Mrs. Jane Washington, his widow, was mistress of the estate. At her death in 1855 her son, John Augustine Washington, became possessor.

Neglect, indifference, and shiftless management now witnessed this once baronial estate going to decay. But some forty years ago the women of the United States came to the rescue of the home and tomb of Washington, and the Mount Vernon Ladies' Association was incorporated, the mansion and two hundred acres passing into its hands for the sum of two hundred thousand dollars.

The present ownership and administration secure the mansion from unnecessary ravages of time and spoliation and vandalism of unworthy visitors. Each room in the main building having been assigned to a State, the lady regent of the State intrusted with its care supervising its restoration, preservation, and appropriate furnishing. In this way the rooms have been brought back in the style of the life of Washington and fitted up either with furniture used by Washington or of his times. The largest room, usually called the banquet-hall or state dining-room, is now known as the New York Room. Rembrandt Peale's "Washington before Yorktown" hangs on the west side of the room. It was given by the artist's heirs to the Mount Vernon Association. Washington is on horseback, and with him are Lafayette, Hamilton, King, Lincoln, and

Rochambeau. The picture is framed in the wood of a tree that grew on the farm of Robert Morris. The military equipments used by Washington in the Braddock campaign are shown in a glass case. The only interesting thing in the New York Room, not a Washington relic, is an old British flag that belonged to General Grant. It is red silk, and so very old that it is quite in tatters, and to preserve it the Regents have had it mounted on plush and framed.

The Washington family dining-room is now the South Carolina Room. The sideboard in this room is a veritable relic, used by Washington and his wife at Mount Vernon. It was presented by the wife of General Robert E. Lee, who wished it to go back in its original place.

Perhaps the most interesting relics in the house are those in the sleeping-chambers. "Lafayette's Room" has still the original four-poster, with heavy tester and hangings, and the desk and dressing-table, which served the marquis on his visits to the Washington family. The room of Nellie Custis has in it a quaint and beautiful chair which came

over with Lord Baltimore, and the mirror
at which she made her toilet and the steps
by which she climbed into her lofty, curtained bed are still in their old places.   In
another room is a curious candlestick of
Mrs. Washington's, an upright rod support-
ing a sliding cross-beam, in each end of
which is a brass candlestick, the base of
which, a tripod, rests upon the floor.   However, the interest of the whole house centres
in the room where Washington died, and in
which the years have wrought no change.
The bed in which he breathed his last holds
its old place, and beside it is the light-stand,
on which are the rings left by his medicine-
glasses, unchanged since that day.   The
secretary at which he wrote, the hair-covered
trunk in which he carried his possessions,
the surveyor's tripod he had used, the cloak
he threw about his shoulders when he went
over the farm, the leathern chair in which he
sat, are all there; and standing in that room
one comes closer to the living presence of
Washington than in any other place on
earth.

A delightful sail takes the visitor from

Mount Vernon to Alexandria, the quiet riverside hamlet which knew Washington as townsman and neighbor. Man and town came into active life together, for it was while Washington was passing from childhood into youth at Mount Vernon that the hamlet of Belhaven grew into the shire town of Alexandria.

Young George rode into town almost daily when at Mount Vernon, and when, his days as a surveyor ended, he was commissioned major in the colonial militia and appointed adjutant of the frontier district, he established his head-quarters at Alexandria, from this centre organizing the militia of the border counties, selecting drill-masters for the officers, attending and regulating musters, and thus slowly yet surely developing that command of detail and talent for organization which five-and-twenty years later transformed on Boston Heights a crude militia into a Continental army. From Alexandria, in April, 1754, a little army of one hundred and fifty men, with Washington at their head, marched off into the wilderness, with their faces turned towards the Ohio River.

In August the remnant came back from the campaign. They had been forced to surrender to the French at Fort Necessity, but had marched out with the honors of war. They went into camp at Alexandria, awaiting orders, and it was at this time an incident occurred which in its sequel proved that Washington had already not only learned how to command men, but had become master of himself as well.

A bitter and exciting contest was in progress for the election of a member for the House of Burgesses. The contestants were Colonel George Fairfax and Mr. Elzey. Washington was a zealous supporter of his friend Fairfax, and in a dispute with a Mr. Payne, who was a small man, but stout-hearted and brave, he grossly insulted Payne, who promptly knocked him down with a hickory stick. He was stunned, and recovered consciousness just in time to prevent serious bloodshed. Several of his subordinate officers being present, they were about to demolish the Payne party, when he checked his angry comrades. Within a short time the regiment received news in their camp that their colonel had been knocked down. On they came with a rush into the town; but a few words from their commander, assuring them he was not hurt and that he had provoked the punishment he got, induced them to return to their quarters. The next day he sent for Payne, who came expecting serious results, but Washington offered his hand.

"Mr. Payne," said he, "I find I was wrong yesterday, but I wish to be right to-day. You have had some satisfaction; and if you think that sufficient, here is my hand. Let us be friends."

Years after the same Mr. Payne had occasion to visit Mount Vernon. "As I drew near," said he, in narrating the incident, "I felt a rising fear lest he should call to mind the blow I had given him in former days," but Washington met him cordially at the door, led him to the presence of Mrs. Washington, and introduced him. "Here, my dear," said he, "here is the little man you have so often heard me talk of, and who, on a difference between us one day, had the resolution to knock me down, big

234

as I am. I know you will honor him as he deserves, for I assure you Mr. Payne has the heart of a true Virginian."

It was at Alexandria that, in 1755, Braddock, with Washington as aide-de-camp, made ready for his disastrous Western campaign, the half-built town becoming for the time the centre of British authority in America. Braddock left Alexandria on April 20; on July 9 he fell, and Washington, filling the mountain passes with troops, saved his fellow-colonials from ravishment by the French and Indians. Soon after this came the young colonel's marriage to the widow Custis, his resignation from the militia, the French power in Virginia being now broken, and his election to the House of Burgesses. At the same time he took an active interest in the concerns of the town growing up on the borders of his estate. He was made a member of the town council in 1766, and about the same time built an office in the village,—torn down only a few years before the Civil War,—where he transacted his business and met his friends. He was also vestryman of the parish which included

Alexandria, helped to build Christ Church in 1769, and worshipped there until his death.

Following the opening of the Revolution, Washington was, of course, absent from Alexandria for many years, but when he returned from the war at Christmas, 1783, the mayor met him with an address, and thenceforth he never left home on a public mission that kindly official addresses were not exchanged with that functionary and the commonalty. Nor did the burden of weightier duties prevent him from at once resuming a helpful interest in the growth and welfare of the town. As soon as he had time to look into its affairs, he found that the lack of avenues of internal trade and the competition of the low Maryland tariff at Georgetown were crippling Alexandria. Accordingly, he at once undertook the removal of these obstructions. He helped to organize the Potomac Company, —since merged into the Chesapeake and Ohio Canal Company,—which built locks around the Potomac Falls, and to avoid the discrimination which the lower duties at

Georgetown made against Alexandria, he led the way to the appointment of commissioners from the two States to settle inter-State difficulties. These commissioners met at Alexandria in March, 1785, and agreed to a uniform tariff to be supported by a naval force in the Chesapeake. This was thought to invade the rights of Pennsylvania and Delaware, whose waters emptied into Chesapeake Bay, and a further conference was invited at Annapolis. Here the delegates discovered that a "more perfect union" was needed, and they called the Constitutional Convention which met at Philadelphia in 1787. Thus Alexandria claims, and rightfully, to be the cradle of the Constitution.

Soon after this, however, the town sunk into the heavy sleep that still locks it in its restful embrace, and looking from the river at its gray-black roofs, gabled, hipped, and gambreled, and covered with shingles put on before the century was young and now warped and moss-grown, or wandering through its ancient streets, cobble-paved and with grass growing all about, one loves to think that Alexandria has changed but little since Washington saw it for the last time. That was on election day in the late November of 1799, and the general, as was his custom, came early to vote. Access to the polls was by a flight of steps outside. These in the year named had become old and shaky, and when Washington reached them, he placed one foot upon them and shook the crazy ascent as if to try its strength. Instantly twenty stout arms, one above the other, grasped the stairway, and a dozen men's shoulders braced it. Nor did a man move until the venerable chief deposited his vote and returned. "I saw his last bow," said one of them in after-years, "and it was more than kingly."

Four weeks later the cold caught during a winter's ride over his estates had done its work, and Washington had become the noblest memory in our history.

CHAPTER XV

THE James, between Richmond and the sea, is a tawny and sluggish stream, fringed with willow and cypress and shut in by low-lying mead and meadow, but it flows through a land rich in memories of a noble and stirring past,—a land where Englishmen first made successful lodgement on New World soil, where amid their rich acres dwelt and ruled those Cavalier planters who were princes in all save the name, and where in later years marched and fought the armies of three great wars. Shirley and Westover, Berkeley and Brandon,—what a quaint and pleasant sound all these names have!—break the storied way to the site of vanished Jamestown, and thence with historic Williamsburg lying between, it is but little more than a score of miles to Yorktown, scene of Cornwallis's surrender and birthplace of a nation.

It was on a clear, balmy morning of the early spring that we left Richmond and drifted slowly down the James on the pleasurable pilgrimage that was to end three days later at Yorktown. Soon the spires and roofs of the sloping seven-hilled city fading into the fleecy western sky were lost to view, and the steamer at the end of an hour came about abreast of Drewry's Bluff, or Fort Darling, its crest flanked with earthworks, now silent, grass-grown, and dismantled, but thirty-five years ago the challenge and menace of the Federal gunboats lying below.

Then Drewry's Bluff also drifted astern, and the boat pushing leisurely ahead passed another reminder of the Civil War,—Dutch Gap, a canal several hundred feet in length, cut by Butler when ascending the river with his gunboats in order to avoid a horseshoe of seven miles. Other interesting memories cling to the narrow peninsula thus converted into an island, for it was here that, in 1612, Sir Thomas Dale laid out a town, defended by palisades and watch-towers, which in honor of the then Prince of Wales he called the City of Henricus. However, no vestige remains of the city or of the "university" established there in the days when Henricus still gave promise of prosperity and greatness.

A little way below the site of hopeful Sir Thomas's lost village is Varina,—the Aiken's Landing of the Civil War,—where Pocahontas passed a part of her brief married life, and then a halt is made at Shirley, a typical manor-house of the middle colonial period, long the lordly home of the Carter family, whose members, intermarrying with the Byrds, the Wickhams, and the Randolphs, played their part, and a worthy one, in the life and history of their time. The olden James River planters built for the future as well as for the present, and Shirley, although erected before the eighteenth century was born, bears well its weight of years. At once massive and simple in design, with foundation-walls from three to four feet in thickness, it is a square, three-storied structure, built of alternating glazed and dull brick, and with sharp-sloping roof cut by dormer-windows. Broad stone steps lead up to the doorways, and spacious porticoes, one of them rising to the second story, flank the eastern and western sides of the house. Brick was also used in the construction of the several outbuildings, arranged in a hollow square, perhaps for purposes of defence in case of attack, and even the dovecote, a peak-roofed turret set upon the ground, is of the same durable material.

The founder of Shirley—he sleeps beneath a massive tomb in the family burial-ground not far from the mansion—was Edward Hill, "Collonel and Commander in Chiefe of the Countys of Charles City and Surrey, Judge of his Majestye's high Court of Admiralty, and Sometime Treasurer of Virginia." His portrait, preserved at Shirley, shows us a handsome, masterful man clad in crimson velvet, lace, and a flowing peruke, and, if the limner painted true, the charm of physical beauty was also the portion of his granddaughter, who gave her heart and hand to a member of the Carter family, in whose possession Shirley and its broad acres have ever since remained. The mansion's interior corresponds with its exterior, and its wainscoted walls boast other portraits than those just mentioned. Carters, Byrds, and Randolphs give silent greeting to the visitor, nor should mention be omitted of a fine replica of Peale's full-length portrait of Washington standing out against the smoke and tumult of a battle scene. The owners of Shirley take pardonable pride in its history and careful preservation, and with its wide-spreading lawn, its curious box-hedged garden, and its pleasing Old World air, it promises to long remain a rare and eloquent survival of the colonial era.

Across the James from Shirley is City Point, the port of Petersburg, and destined to remain forever celebrated for its part in the Civil War. Here was enacted the closing act of the great drama, and there stands on the summit of the steep bluff, at the base of which the Appomattox joins the James, the low, rambling, bullet-riddled house used as head-quarters by General Grant at that time. Near City Point once stood the manor-house of Cawsons, the birthplace of brilliant and hapless John Randolph, whose home in later years we shall come upon at

another stage of our pilgrimage. Cawsons was destroyed early in the century, but
the Randolphs were at one time the owners
of vast estates along the James and the
Appomattox, and the whole region about
City Point is indissolubly bound up with
their name.

Westover House, another splendid reminder of colonial Virginia, comes into
view soon after passing City Point. The
patent of Westover was originally granted
to the Pawlet family, and sold by Sir John
Pawlet, in 1665, to Theodore Bland, whose
tomb and armorial bearings may still be seen
on the estate. From Bland's descendants
it passed by purchase to the Byrds, and with
the name of Colonel William Byrd, second
of that line in America, it is now invariably
associated. The first William Byrd was a
shrewd young Cheshireman, who secured
from the crown a grant of land covering
nearly the whole sight of modern Richmond
and of Manchester on the opposite bank of
the James. There he built for himself a
fortified dwelling, which he called Belvidere,
and throve so well in his new home that

when he died, in 1704, he left his son and namesake one of the richest men in the colonies.

To this second William Byrd, educated in England and there called to the bar of the Middle Temple, was reserved a brilliant and exceptional career, as courtier, author, traveller, and patron of the arts, fairly entitling him to high rank among the leaders of his time, and eloquently epitomized in the stately periods of the inscription upon the shaft above his grave in the rear of Westover House. "Eminently fitted," this inscription tells us, " for the service and ornament of his country, he was made Receiver general of his Majesty's revenues here,"—an office his father had held before him,—" was thrice appointed publick agent to the Court and ministry of England, and being thirty-seven years a member at last became President of the Council of this Colony. To all this were added a great elegancy of taste and life, the well-bred gentleman and polite companion, the splendid Oeconomist and prudent father of a family, with the constant enemy of all exhorbitant power and hearty friend to the liberties of his country."

Truly a remarkable man to merit an eulogium of this sort, but contemporary records prove that Colonel Byrd deserved it. He was thirty years of age when he became master of Westover, where his father had builded and dwelt during the closing years of his life, and, save for occasional absences in England, he resided there until his death in 1744, dispensing a royal hospitality and playing an active and sagacious part in public affairs, ever ready with pen, purse, and brain to serve his king and his province. He was one of the commissioners who, in 1728, fixed the boundary-line between North Carolina and Virginia, and five years later he laid out near his father's little fortress of Belvidere a town "to be called Richmond," thus giving a site and name to Virginia's present capital.

The sprightly Marquis de Chastellux, visiting Westover in 1782, wrote of it as "surpassing all other estates on the river in the magnificence of its buildings, the beauty of its situation, and the pleasures of its society,"

and the latter-day visitor finds no cause to
quarrel with this description. The present
mansion, restored in 1749 by the son and
namesake of the second William Byrd, is
a substantial three-story structure, situated,
perhaps, a hundred yards from the river's
bank; fronted by a broad, closely-kept lawn,
and with a line of noble trees caressing the
dormer-windows of its roof. At each end
of the grounds are elaborate gates of ham-
mered iron, with the arms of the Byrd family curiously inwrought, and there is yet a
third gate, above which perch leaden eagles
with outstretched wings, larger and more
elaborate in decoration, and capable of giving entrance to the most ponderous chariot.
Everything else is on the same lordly scale.
Moreover, by its present proprietor, one of
the most successful planters in the State,
Westover has been restored to much of its
pristine dignity. And what stirring days
the old house has seen! Bacon and his men,
bivouacking here on their daring forays
against the Indians, ate, drank, slept upon
their arms, and rode away; Benedict Arnold, on his way to capture Richmond, in

1781, landed and slept at Westover, and in the old nursery on the ground-floor Cornwallis quartered the horses of his troopers, while, during the Civil War, several generals of the Union army, notably McClellan, made their head-quarters at the mansion so popular with the soldiers of earlier revolutions.

As Westover recalls the Byrds, so Berkeley on the north side of the James, and Brandon and Upper Brandon on the south, stand as monuments to the American Harrisons. Upper Brandon is still occupied by a representative of the original family, but has never fully recovered from the shocks and ravages of the Civil War. Brandon, erected in 1725, and the birthplace of the first President Harrison, also suffered heavily in war-time, but is still one of the most delectable nooks in the Old Dominion. It has remained in the Harrison family since its foundation. Fronting a sweep of the James two miles wide, a broad avenue, with an old-fashioned border of box, leads from the house to Brandon wharf. On either side of this avenue is an extensive lawn, dotted with flowers, shrubs, and trees. In the middle of the irregular brick structure is the oldest part of Brandon House, built of English brick by the father of Colonel Benjamin Harrison, signer of the Declaration of Independence, and friend of Washington. This part is two stories and a half high. Antique dormer-windows are on the top of the slanting roof, and four round brick columns support the roof of the porches, which are of the same height as the two stories, and which ornament both the river and landward entrances to the house. Brandon House took its name from the Duchess of Brandon, friend and kinswoman of the first Harrison of Brandon. Additions have been made to the house from time to time. Two wings connected with the main building by long halls, one used as a billiard-room and the other as a tenpin-alley, now constitute the entire house, which contains fifteen large rooms, and is partly enveloped in a luxuriant growth of ivy.

On entering the house one finds himself in a large square hall hung with stag-horns, rusty old swords, ancient-looking guns, and other implements of hunting and warfare. This opens on one side to a drawing-room of magnificent proportions; on the other to an equally large dining-room, both filled with handsome old furniture, some of which antedates the Revolution, the sideboard in the dining-room being weighted down with silver of a unique and ancient pattern. Hung in these two rooms are Brandon's rarest treasures,—its family portraits. Some of these are of unusual interest, and several were painted from life by Sir Peter Lely. The collection includes the portraits gathered by Colonel William Byrd, whose son married a daughter of Benjamin Harrison, which when Westover was sold were conveyed to Brandon. Among these portraits is one of the Duke of Albemarle, painted by Sir Peter Lely; one of Colonel William Byrd, and another of the beautiful Evelyn Byrd, one of Virginia's old-time belles. She was beloved by the Earl of Peterborough, but her father opposed the marriage, and she died young. Tradition says that her heart was broken. Between her portrait and that of Lady Betty Claypole, daughter of Oliver Cromwell, hangs a fine portrait of Colonel Benjamin Harrison, taken when he was a delicate, slender-looking young man.

On the opposite wall is a portrait of Mrs. Benjamin Harrison, who was Miss Anne Randolph, painted by Sir Thomas Lawrence. In the dining-room are portraits of Lord Fairfax, Sir Robert Southwell, Sir Robert Walpole, the Duke of Orrery, and the Duchess of Brandon. The walls of both rooms are literally covered with pictures, including besides those mentioned interesting portraits of many of the Harrisons and Randolphs of past generations. The library is in one wing of the house, and contains a large collection of rare books. The Byrd Memoirs in manuscript, beautifully bound, give almost a complete history of early Virginia, and a turning of their quaintly-worded pages is one of the many pleasures that falls to the lot of the pilgrim so fortunate as to become the guest of the present gracious mistress of Brandon House.

Our river journey had fit ending at the site of ancient Jamestown, on what was once a peninsula, but is now an island in the James. At the present time all that remains of the first successful English colony in America are a neglected graveyard and the crumbling walls of a ruined church, but the charm Jamestown still holds for the visitor is unique and lasting. The little church now in ruins was built in 1609. Here often came to worship Captain John Smith, Admiral of New England and doughty slayer of Turks, and those hopeful yet unruly followers whom he taught to earn their bread by the sweat of their brows, and within its walls pious Robert Hunt, the first English-speaking missionary to preach the gospel of Christ in America,—let his name be ever honored!—joined the " good and blessed" Pocahontas in wedlock to the young and handsome planter, John Rolfe. Privations overcame Hunt, and he died three years after he landed with Smith at Jamestown, but the church of which he was the first pastor continued to be used as a house of worship until the civil war which ended in the execution of Charles I., during which, together with Jamestown, it fell into the

RUINED TOWER OF JAMESTOWN CHURCH.

hands of Bacon and his rebel followers, and was fired, though not totally destroyed.

All about the site of vanished Jamestown Nature for two centuries has been slowly yet steadily reclaiming her own. Not far from the ruined church we came upon a few old slabs which mark the resting-place of some of the Jamestown pioneers, most of whom died during the first twenty years of the colony's history. These stones, moss-grown and black with age, have been cracked and riven by the roots of the trees spreading under them, and with the inscriptions, save in one or two instances, no longer legible, serve only to add to the romance of the place.

A little way from this burial-ground is the only other remaining relic of Jamestown, —the great house built by Sir William Berkeley, and now the home of the owner and postmistress, as she is also the sole white inhabitant of Jamestown Island. In this house Berkeley lived for thirty years as royal governor, and here, like the narrow-minded and self-satisfied bigot that he was, he sat down, and thanking God that there were

no printing-presses in America, beseeched
Him that none might be suffered to enter
for centuries to come. Berkeley was driven
from his home by Bacon and his men, and
came near falling a victim to the progressive
spirit against which he had fought and
prayed, but in the end he reëstablished his
government at Williamsburg, and Charles
II., in staying all too tardily the bloody
hands of the old man's blind revenge, cyni-
cally declared that the governor had hanged
more men in the Virginia wilderness for
abetting Bacon than he himself had put to
death for the murder of his father, Charles I.

Other shades than those of Smith and
Berkeley haunt this island of Jamestown.
"There were brave men before Agamem-
non," and it is now known that eighty years
before the arrival of the English it was the
site of an attempted settlement by the Span-
iards. Recent researches in the royal library at Simancas in Spain have disclosed
that in the summer of 1526 one Lucas Vas-
quez de Ayllon, a Spanish captain who " as-
pired to the glory of discovering some new
land and making it the seat of a prosperous

colony," sailed from San Domingo with three large ships and six hundred persons of both sexes, and, after touching on what is now the South Carolina shore, entered and proceeded up the James. Fifty miles from its mouth he landed, and on the future site of Jamestown founded a settlement which he christened San Miguel de Guandope. But ill-luck from the first attended the venture. De Ayllon died in October, 1626; his followers mutinied against their new commander, and the colony was speedily abandoned. Less than a quarter of the colonists in the end regained the island of San Domingo. The rest had died of fever, cold, and privation. The tender carrying De Ayllon's body foundered at sea, and the ocean rolls above the resting-place of the adventurer whose keel had tracked its waters in profitless quest of wealth, fame, and honors.

Leaving Jamestown Island, where our stay had been made doubly pleasant by the generous welcome of its owner, we crossed to the north shore, and took carriage for the drive over a cool forest road to Williamsburg,—long the colonial capital of Virginia and the site of old William and Mary College. It is hardly too much to say of it that it is the most charmingly antique town in America,—certainly it is the most charming in the Old Dominion. Duke of Gloucester is the name of the main street of the village, which broadens at its centre into an open square called Court-House Green, where stands an ancient temple of justice, modelled by the graceful hand of Sir Christopher Wren, and surrounded by fine colonial residences, among them those of John Randolph and Beverly Tucker, and Chancellor Wythe's old house, where his wicked nephew poisoned him. Farther up Duke of Gloucester Street is another square—Palace Green —faced by other historic mansions, including the old palace of the royal governors and the house used by Washington as his head-quarters just before the siege of Yorktown.

Nearly opposite to Palace Green is the powder-magazine of colonial days, in appearance very like the Martello towers at Quebec, save that it is octagonal instead of round. It is called the " Powder-Horn," and was built by Sir Alexander Spotswood, the deputy or lieutenant of George Hamilton, Earl of Orkney, governor and commander-in-chief of the colony. There had been great rejoicing in the colony when Governor Spotswood arrived, because he brought with him the habeas corpus act. This act had been refused by the governors at times when their deputies had taken it on themselves to exercise it on their own authority. So it was a matter of rejoicing when a deputy came bringing it in his own name. However, it was not long before there was an open quarrel between Spotswood and the House of Burgesses, because they would not grant certain money that he asked for necessary defence. Two years later, having gained the confidence of the people by his wise measures, the Assembly granted him all he asked, and in 1714 the statute was passed ordering the erection of the magazine.

Sixty years later the " Powder-Horn" became the scene of the first overt act of the Revolution. In the winter of 1775, when

the clouds of war were gathering thick and
fast, a plan was formed by the royal author-
ities to disarm all the colonies. In pursuit
of this plan, on the night of April 20, 1775,
a number of marines, who had been concealed in the palace at Williamsburg, moved
the powder from the magazine to the " Magdalen," a man-of-war on the James River.
The removal of the powder was discovered
by the citizens early in the morning. Duke
of Gloucester Street was crowded at once,
and threats were made. A deputation was
sent to the palace demanding the return of
the powder. They found the place in a
state of defence, many arms lying around.
Lord Dunmore, the governor, gave some
untruthful excuse, and pledged his honor
that if the powder was needed in Williamsburg it should be returned in half an hour.
The news of the removal of the powder
spread like wildfire. Patrick Henry raised
three hundred men, " Hanover Volunteers,"
and marched towards Williamsburg, their
numbers increasing as they went. Dunmore was obliged to go to meet them and

to compromise the matter by paying for the powder.

The House of Burgesses assembled on June 1, 1775. Lord Dunmore made a polite address and presented Lord North's "Conciliatory Plan." A committee was appointed to report upon it, and Thomas Jefferson was selected to write the report. Suddenly, from a most unexpected quarter, on June 5, came a sound that ended all discussion. On that night some young men went to the magazine to procure arms. Lord Dunmore had before this delivered up the keys of the magazine. They unlocked the door, and as they pushed it open it pulled a concealed cord that discharged a spring-gun. Three of the young men were wounded. The Assembly was aroused to intense excitement. Persons were officially appointed to examine the magazine. It was done cautiously, and under the floor several barrels of powder were found buried. Duke of Gloucester Street was again crowded by excited citizens, and again threats were made. Before the day dawned Lord Dunmore and family had fled to the man-of-war "Fowey" at

Yorktown, never to return to Williamsburg, and the disputed powder, seized without delay by the colonists, was put to use in the war that followed, while Patrick Henry was speedily installed in Dunmore's place as the first governor of the State of Virginia.

Turning from the "Powder-Horn," now owned and kept in repair by the women of Williamsburg, the next place of interest reached in our leisurely ramble down Duke of Gloucester Street was the ancient, ivy-hidden church of Bruton parish,—the oldest Protestant house of worship in use in America. It is built in shape of a cross, and was planned by Sir Christopher Wren. It stands in the midst of a beautiful grove of elms, surrounded by tombs and monuments of the dead, as if dreaming of the faded glories of the past. Williamsburg people tell you that Queen Anne went to see the bell for its tower cast and threw her silver ornaments in the molten bronze. Many curious things are seen in and near this old church. In a house across the Green are kept the communion services given by Queen Anne and George III., and in the church itself is placed the font which held the water into which the minister dipped his fingers when he baptized Pocahontas. In its floor are tablets over graves showing that lords, dukes, knights, and chancellors are resting there, among them a modern slab to the memory of the Confederates who were killed in the battle of Williamsburg. " They died for us" it is here declared. Theodore Winthrop, of Massachusetts, it will be remembered, fell in that battle, and his body rested for several years in Bruton church-yard, among the graves of colonial worthies whom Virginians still delight to honor.

At the end of Duke of Gloucester Street stands the restored and lately reopened William and Mary College. The second college in America, Harvard having been the first, it was chartered in 1691, Queen Mary persuading her husband to endow it with two thousand pounds per year in money, twenty thousand acres of land, and one penny per pound upon all the tobacco exported from Maryland and Virginia, together with all the fees and profits arising from the office of surveyor-general, which was to be controlled by the president and faculty. In 1698 the college building, planned by Wren, was finished and the new seat of learning named William and Mary, in honor of the generous king and queen. For many years thereafter it was the centre of intellectual life in the Old Dominion. Three Presidents were graduated within its walls and one chief-justice, and many other distinguished men can claim it as their alma mater.

The college buildings were burned in 1705. They were rebuilt at once, but were burned again and again, the last time in 1862. However, the fires that have afflicted the college buildings have spared the famous college statue, and it stands serenely in the middle of the college green. Norborne Berkeley, Baron de Botetourt, governor-general of Virginia, arrived at Hampton Roads, eight weeks out from Portsmouth, in October, 1768, and so pleased the people of the colony that they soon afterwards erected a marble statue to him in front of the college. It represents him in court dress with a short sword by his side, and, although it has suffered some degree of mutilation, it still is a fine specimen of the sculptor's art. William and Mary during the last half-century has had a checkered history. Some years ago it had dwindled to proportions that threatened its speedy death, but more recently has taken new lease of life, and now promises a long future of usefulness.

At the other end of Duke of Gloucester Street, one mile distant from the college, is the site of the old House of Burgesses. Nothing is left of it save the foundation of bricks and masses of broken plaster from its walls. It was here that Henry's eloquence competed with Otis's at Boston for the rank of first orator of the Revolution, and it was here occurred a most interesting episode in the life of Washington. For faithful performance of public duties the House of Burgesses voted him a splendid sword and belt, and they were presented by Edmund Randolph, then president of the House, in an eloquent and impressive speech, which so overcame young Washington that in his effort to reply he could not utter a word. Randolph came to his rescue. " Sit down,

Mr. Washington," said he, " your modesty is only equalled by your bravery, and that very far surpasses any words I have to express it."

Close to the site of the old Capitol is the famous Red Lion Hotel, a long building with hip-roof and dormer-windows, now far gone in the process of decay. Near by is the site of the Raleigh Tavern, which Williamsburg people say was a grand place. Nothing can now be seen of this famous old tavern except the foundation of the massive pillars which supported its piazza, it having been pulled down years ago and a large brick store built upon the site. It was in the ballroom of this Raleigh Tavern that Patrick Henry made his great speech denouncing British wrongs placed upon her colonies, and in its delivery won for himself a place among the master orators of all time.

Those were Williamsburg's palmiest days, but when the capital was moved to Richmond in 1779 the town's glory was taken from it. Yet it has not suffered decay. Indeed, it has accomplished one of the most difficult things in the life of man or town, for it has fallen gracefully into mossy age. Beauty and quiet now brood over it, and we found a single afternoon of spring all too short a time to idle among its ancient houses or linger under the stately elms that give graceful shade to Court and Palace Greens, but time pressed, and under the mellow glow of a westering sun we left Williamsburg behind us and took to the winding road, which ere night came on led us to the broad estuary of the York River and to Yorktown, another sleepy old village that seems by some miracle to have escaped the influence of the nineteenth century.

Little York, now nearing the end of its second century of existence, was never a populous place even when it thrived the most, but it was the political and trading centre of one of the eight boroughs into which Virginia was originally divided, and during the sixty years immediately preceding the Revolution an influential factor in the direction of affairs. The town's first settler was Thomas Nelson, a canny Scotch trader, who established there a store which for two generations yielded to those called by his

name a never-ending harvest of golden
guineas. This store was destroyed during
the war of 1812, but the custom-house
where the Nelsons' goods were entered—
it was, it is said, the first of its kind erected
in America—still stands near the water
front, with moss-covered roof, thick walls,
and massive oaken doors and shutters.

Less than a stone's throw away stands the
dwelling, with its lofty chimneys and solid
walls, builded by Scotch Tom when riches
had come to him with age, after which he
died and was buried,—his tomb remains
one of the notable relics of the village,—but
not until he had founded a family from
which issued in the third generation General
Thomas Nelson, one of the most brilliant
of that body of great men who stand a splendid cluster of stars against the early dawn
of the country's history. This Thomas Nelson, third of the name, though educated
at Eton and Cambridge, when the Revolution came joined the side of the ultra patriots, was a conspicuous member of all the
decisive conventions, and as a delegate to
that of 1776 signed the great Declaration.

Finally, in 1780, he succeeded Henry as governor of his State, with almost dictatorial power to manage both her military and civil policy. "His popularity was unbounded," says the historian, and, he might have added, so were the general's patriotism and generosity, for when, Virginia's credit being low, money was wanted to pay the troops and run the government, Nelson borrowed millions on his personal security and went on; and again, when regiments mutinied and refused to march, he raised money and paid them, although in so doing he wrecked his own and his children's fortunes.

Recalling the career of this uncommon man, one rejoices that the triumphant close of the seven years' struggle in which he bore so fine a part was pitched at the place most closely associated with his name and fame. The story of what happened at Yorktown in the fall of 1781 grows more lustrous with the years. Only a few months before the patriot cause had seemed a doubtful if not a hopeless one. The army of the South had been defeated and driven back into Virginia, only by forced marches escaping complete destruction; Virginia, the backbone of the Revolution, had been swept by two invasions; and Cornwallis with his army was marching triumphantly through her borders, trying by every means he could devise to bring his only opponent, the youthful Lafayette, to an engagement. Had the French officer proved as reckless as the British commander believed him, the end would have come before De Grasse with his fleet anchored in the Chesapeake. He was no novice in the art of war, however, and at length Cornwallis, wearied of trying to catch him, retired to Yorktown, and intrenching himself, awaited reënforcements from the North.

It was at this critical moment that kindly Providence directed the French admiral to the Virginia coast, and Washington, finding himself possessed of a force such as he had never hoped for in his wildest dreams, and knowing that he could count on the new reënforcements for only a few weeks, resolved to put his fate to the touch and win if possible by a single bold cast of the die. Accordingly, he withdrew from New York and came down to Jersey as if to get near his ovens, a move which so misled the British commander that he did not suspect its ulterior object until he learned that the patriot army was well on its way to Virginia. In the last days of September the American commander arrived before Yorktown and began a siege memorable for the bravery and determination with which it was prosecuted.

The expected relief did not come to Cornwallis, and ere the end of the third week his troops marched out with cased colors, prisoners of war. A monument, unveiled with imposing ceremonies some years ago, now marks the spot where this event took place, and a short way from the town still stands the old weather-beaten mansion known as the Moore House, in the sitting-room of which were drawn up the articles of capitulation of the British army. This house, now tenantless and falling into decay, was historical even then, for it had been the country residence of Governor Spotswood, who, as the great Marlborough's aide-de-camp, had carried the news of Blenheim to England, and who later had come to the Old Dominion to rule it for a time with a soldier's courage and decision and the foresight of a statesman able to see beyond the fret of small minds over little things.

The Nelson House, used by Cornwallis as his head-quarters during the last days of the siege, after his first had been shelled to pieces, still bears the iron scars made by the American cannon, pointed at it by order of General Nelson, who when told that the British general was lodged there, offered five guineas to the gunners for every shot which should strike it. Otherwise it is well preserved; and what a glorious company of shades haunt its high wainscoted rooms! Washington and Mason and Jefferson received cordial welcome from its master, while Lafayette, returning in his old age, the honored and revered guest of the mighty nation he had helped to create, slept here and added another to the many associations which already surrounded the mansion.

Growth and activity went out from York-town along with the patriot troopers, and to-day, with its few old brick houses scattered among modern shanties, it is the sleepiest of sleepy villages,—a place where modest poverty dwells content and strife and hurry are alien things. Peaceful be its slumbers amid green and quiet fields, for it has well earned the rest that is the right of honored age.

INDEX

A

Abercrombie, General, head-
quarters of, i. 117, 120
Accomac, county of, ii. 15
county seat of, ii. 19
Acker, Woolfert, i. 147
Adams, John, ii. 53, 65
inauguration of, ii. 72, 73
Adams, Samuel, ii. 53, 65
Agnew, General, ii. 70
Aiken's Landing, ii. 141
Albany, a journey to, i. 220
a rendezvous, i. 120
Broadway in, i. 116
from New York to, i. 142
settlement of, i. 111–113
Albemarle, Duke of, ii. 250
Alexandria, ii. 179, 206
centre of British authority,
ii. 235
growth of, ii. 236, 237
head-quarters at, ii. 232
incident in camp at, ii, 233
Washington votes in, ii.
238
Algonquins, i. 174
dwelling-place of, i. 209
Allen, William, ii. 51
Alps, i. 131
Alston, Washington, i. [217,
218
Alva, i. 212
Amana, ii. 173
community of, ii. 196–205
Amsterdam, Golden's yard
in, i. 84
Anastasia, Sister. See
Tabea, Sister.

André, Major, tragedy of, i.
153, 154, 237–239
Annapolis, i. 83
and Philadelphia, travel
between, ii. 40
conference at, ii. 237
Anne, Queen, i. 134, 176 ; ii.
53, 260
Anthony, Captain, ii. 30
Anthony's Nose, i. 158, 223
Anti-rent war, i. 113–115
Appomattox, ii. 243
Arlington, ii. 12, 13, 19
Armstrong, John, i. 125
old home of, i. 132
Arnold, Benedict, i. 80, 153
army of, i. 197, 237 ; ii. 24
Arthur, Chester A., last
home of, i. 95
Asbury, i. 136
Assateague, ii. 20
Astor, John Jacob, i. 89
last home of, i. 97
Audubon, i. 106, 107
Audubon mansion, changes
in, i. 108
first telegraph used in,
i. 107
Audubon Park, i. 106, 107
Auriesville, i. 176
history of, i. 178

B

Babylon, i. 66
"Bachelor," the barque, i.
15
Bacon, ii. 247, 254
Baden, ii. 156

INDEX

Baerren Island, i. 112
Baker, R. L., 182
Ball, Nicholas, i. 32, 33
Baltimore, ii. 24
Baltimore, Lord, ii. 37
Bancroft, George, i. 28, 132
Bard, Samuel, Dr., i. 170
Bartram, John, a botanist, ii.
    62, 63
    garden of, ii. 60, 61
    house of, ii. 59
Bartram, William, ii. 60
Battery, the, i. 77
    northern boundary of, i.
    81
    promenade, i. 79
    visitors to, i. 80
Baumeler, Joseph, ii. 190,
    191, 194
    marries, ii. 195
Baxter, Philip, odd agree-
    ment of, ii. 220, 221
Baylor's Cavalry, ii. 16
Beecher, Lyman, i. 57
Beekman, Gerard D., Gen-
    eral, i. 154
Behring Strait, ii. 156.
Beissel, Conrad (Father
    Friedsam), confession
    to, ii. 127
    death of, ii. 128, 131, 135
    doctrine of, ii. 123
    founds Order, ii. 119–121
    hymns of, ii. 124, 125
Belhaven, ii. 232
Bell House, the old, ii. 147
Bellomont, Lord, i. 25, 26,
    27
Belvidere, fortress of, ii. 246
Bensons, ii. 44
Berkeley, ii. 239, 248
Berkeley, William, Sir,
    house of, ii. 253
    revenge of, ii. 254
Berkeley, Norborne, Baron
    de Botetourt, ii. 262
Berlin, ii. 22
Bethania, ii. 122
    at the present, ii. 131, 133

Bethlehem, ii. 155
    Christmas celebration at,
    ii. 170–172
    community, ii. 143, 144
    Moravian buildings in, ii.
    145–147
    settlement of, ii. 139, 140,
    142
Bjork, ii. 44
Black Horse Tavern, i. 156,
    157
Bland, Theodore, ii. 244
Block, Adrian, i. 32
Block Island, centre, i. 37–39
    description of, i. 30, 31
    double-ender, i. 34–36
    heading for, i. 29
    history of, i. 32–34
    legends, i. 42–44
    wrecks, i. 41
Block Islanders, i. 44
Blockley Hill, ii. 49
Bloomingdale Road, i. 143
Boehme, ii. 190, 197
Bohemia, i. 137
Bonaparte, Jerome, i. 80
Bordley, John Beale, ii. 32,
    33
Bordley, Margaret Chew, ii.
    32
Boston, i. 21, 140
    heights, ii. 232
    turnpike, i. 172
Botta, Vincenza, Madame, i.
    65
Bowery, i. 78
Bowling Green, i. 77–79
    house of, i. 74
Bowne, John, i. 73
    house of, i. 74
Braddock, i. 86
    campaign of, ii. 235
Brandon, ii. 248
Brandon, Duchess of, ii. 249,
    251
Brandon House, iii. 249
    family portraits of, ii.
    250, 251
Brant, Joseph, picture of, i.
    134, 192

274

INDEX

Brandywine, battle of, ii. 16, 63, 83, 84, 90
Breakneck Hill, i. 143
Brick Meeting-House, Old, ii. 98, 100, 101
Bridgehampton, i. 56
Bridgewater, Duke of, i. 129
Brinley, Grissell. See Sylvester, Grissell (Brinley), Mrs.
Bristol, ii. 75, 76
Bristol Channel, ii. 28
British officer, disinterment of a, i. 144
Broad Street, i. 79
Broadway, i. 78, 81, 143
post road called, i. 144, 145
Bronx, the, i. 137
Brooklyn, i. 67
Bruton Church, ii. 260, 261
Bryant, Fanny, grave of, i. 72, 73
Bryant, William Cullen, i. 65
grave of, i. 72, 73
home of, i. 71, 72
Buffalo, ii. 197
Bunker Hill, ii. 209
Burgoyne, i. 120, 121
descends on New York, i. 192
Burns, heroine of, i. 150
Burr, Aaron, 170
a protégé of, i. 217
marriage of, i. 90–92, 121
Burr, Theodosia, i. 91
Burton, William E., house once owned by, i. 99
Butler, Pennsylvania, ii. 174, 175
Byrd, Evelyn, ii. 250
Byrd family, ii. 241, 244, 247, 248
Byrd, William, ii. 244
Byrd, William (second), Colonel, ii. 244–246
son of, ii. 247

C

Cæsar, story of the slave, i. 152, 153
California, gold in, ii. 156, 157
Calvert, Leonard, Sir, ii. 37
Calvert, Quaker village of, ii. 92, 98–102
Calverts, the, ii. 36, 38
Calvinists, ii. 108
Cambrian Hills, ii. 28
Cambridge, ii. 25, 26
Campbell, Major, i. 161
Canada, i. 175
missionaries from, i. 179
Canajoharie, i. 188, 189, 190
Carey sisters, i. 65
Carolina, North, i. 66
Carpenter Mansion, ii. 49
Carter family, the, ii. 241
Carthagena, ii. 211
Cary, Sally, ii. 214
Castle Garden, i. 79, 80
Catholics, ii. 108
Catskill, town of, i. 209
soldiers of, i. 212, 214, 217
Catskills, i. 173, 207
Cawsons' manor-house, ii. 243
Cayugas, i. 175
Cazenovia, i. 176, 198, 200, 201
Cedarcraft, ii. 96, 97
Cedarmere, i. 71, 72
Cemetery, East Hampton, i. 18
Centreville, ii. 39
Charles I., ii. 254
wife of, ii. 30
Charles XII., ii. 45, 49, 254
"Chasseur," the privateer, ii. 28
Chatham Square, i. 78
Chatham Street, i. 78
Chenango County, i. 200
Chesapeake, ii. 9, 12, 24
naval force in the, ii. 237

INDEX

Fulton, Robert, death of, i. 130, 131
marriage of, i. 130
Fulton, the elder, ii. 103

G

Gage, General, i. 21
Gallows Hill, story of, i. 159, 160
Gansevoort, Peter, Colonel, i. 191, 193, 194
Gardiner, David, i. 17, 19
receives patent, i. 20
Gardiner Greens, i. 28
Gardiner, John I., annoyed by pirates, i. 20, 21
daughter of, i. 28, 29
relations with Captain Kidd, i. 25–27
Gardiner, John Lyon, i. 21
Gardiner, Juliana, i. 28
Gardiner, Lion, i. 14
death of, i. 18, 19, 22
friendship with Wyandance, i. 17
in Connecticut, i. 15
purchases island, i. 16
residence at East Hampton, i. 18
system of, i. 23
Gardiner, Mary, i. 28
Gardiner, Mrs., keeps a diamond, i. 27
receives presents from Kidd, i. 25, 26
Gardiner's Bay, i. 22, 24, 29
Gardiner's Island, i. 13, 16, 45
at the present time, i. 22, 23
disturbed by Captain Kidd, i. 24
in the Revolution, i. 21
manor of, i. 14
title to, i. 20
Gardiners, the, connections of, i. 28

Garretson, Freeborn, i. 125
at Rhinebeck, i. 171
Garretson House, i. 75
Garretsons, residence of the, i. 132
Gates conspiracy, i. 226, 228
Gates, General, i. 227
Genesee country, the, i. 200
Genet, Edmond Charles, citizen, i. 173
Genet, homestead, i. 173
George I., King, i. 122
George III., King, i. 152, 213, 239 ; ii. 206, 260
Georgetown, ii. 236, 237
Germantown, ii. 47
battle of, ii. 16, 69, 83
St. Michael's Church, ii. 71
Girondists, ii. 220
Gist, militiamen under, ii. 16
Glenwood, i. 145, 146
Gloria Dei. See Old Swedes' Church
Goelet, Jane, Miss. See Dies, Madam
Golden Horn, i. 79
Goodwin, Parke, i. 99
Gould, Jay, i. 145
Goupil, Rene, Brother, martyrdom of, i. 179–181, 182
Gouverneur, Samuel L., i. 95
Governor's Creek, ii. 76
Grant, General, home of, i. 96 ; ii. 16, 243
Grant, Mrs., i. 96
Grassmere, i. 32
Gravesend, i. 15
Gray's Ferry Road, ii. 59
Great Plains road, i. 51
Great Queen Street. See Pearl Street
Great South Bay, i. 61
Greeley, Horace, house of, i. 97
Green Thomas, chaplain, i. 27
Greenbush, house in, i. 116, 117

INDEX

Greene, General Nathaniel, i. 40, 88; ii. 84
Greenport, i. 13, 45, 49
Greenwich Street, i. 79
Greenwich village, i. 94
Grey, General, ii. 91
Gulf of Mexico, i. 174
Gunston Hall, ii. 219
Gustavus Adolphus, dream of, ii. 42, 43, 44

H

Hale, Nathan, Captain, capture of, i. 67, 68
"Half Moon," the, i. 111
Half-Way Hollow Hills, i. 66
Hamilton, Alexander, i. 93
  death of, i. 94
  marriage of, i. 121, 125, 170
  trees planted by, i. 94, 95
  visits André, i. 238
Hamilton, George, Earl of Orkney, ii. 257
Hamilton, Governor, ii. 49
Hamilton Grange, i. 93–95
Hamilton, Mrs., i. 94
Hampton Roads, ii. 27, 262
Hamptons, isolated, i. 60
  transfer of the, i. 49, 50
Hancock, John, ii. 53, 66
Hanover Square, i. 81, 82
Hanover Volunteers, ii. 258
Hapsburg, Rudolph of, i. 131
Harmonists, ii. 175
  generosity of, ii. 185
  leave Economy, ii. 178, 179
  present head, ii. 182
  wealth of, ii. 183
Harmony Society, ii. 174
Harrison, Benjamin, Colonel, ii. 249, 251
Harrison, Benjamin, Mrs., ii. 251

Harrison, President (first), ii. 248
Hartford colony, i. 49
Harvard College, ii. 261
Harvey, John, Sir, ii. 36
Hasbrouck, Colonel, house built by, i. 222
Hasbrouck family, i. 225
Hastings, i. 145, 146
Haunted Lake, i. 204, 206
Havana, voyage of a double-ender to, i. 35, 36
Haverstraw Bay, i. 157, 237, 167
Haydn, symphonies of, ii. 167
Heere Graft. See Broad Street
Heinemann, Barbara, ii. 197
Helderbergs, i. 173
Henrici, Jacob, ii. 182, 185
Henricus, City of, ii. 241
Henry, Patrick, ii. 53, 65, 258, 260, 263
  great speech of, ii. 264
Herkimer, Nicholas, General, i. 190, 191
  death of, i. 197
  marches to Fort Schuyler, i. 192–194
  monument to, i. 198
  wounded at Oriskany, i. 195, 196
Herkimer, town of, i. 192
Hermitage, the, ii. 40
Hessian occupation, i. 75
Highlands, i. 158
  trail, i. 159, 162, 165, 166, 233
Hill, Edward, ii. 241
Hohenlinden, ii. 78
Holland and France, smuggling for, ii. 27
  colonists from, i. 111
  windmills from, i. 51
Holland Land Company, i. 200
Hollanders, i. 210
Hollywood Cemetery, i. 96

281

INDEX

Holme, Thomas, ii. 46
Holtenstein, Amos, preacher, baptizes, ii. 116–118
Honorable Society of Carpenters, hall built by, ii. 64, 66
Hopkins, Stephen, ii. 65
Horsford, Eben Norton, i. 48
Hospital, New York, i. 81
Hostetter, a Dunker, ii. 116
House of Burgesses, ii. 235, 257, 259
  site of, ii. 263
  the Beverly Robinson, i. 233
Howard, John Eager, Colonel, granddaughter of, ii. 30
Howe, i. 120
Hudson, Hendrick, i. 111, 172
Hudson Highlands, i. 28
Hudson River, domains, i. 132
  first steamer launched on, i. 124
  literary landmarks of, i. 231
  military works, i. 232
  patroon system introduced on the, i. 111, 112
  poor man's side of the, i. 207–209
  steamboat, i. 218
  Valley, i. 158, 233
  view, i. 120
  villa regions, i. 145
  Washington's retreat across the, i. 87
Hudson River Railroad, i. 142
Huguenots, i. 73–75
Hunt, Robert, ii. 252
Huntingdon Harbor, i. 49, 66–68
  town, i. 66
Huss, John, i. 137

Hyde, Edward, Lord Cornbury, i. 169
Hyde Park, i. 169

I

Idele, i. 132
Idlewild, i. 230
Indian Brook, i. 156
Indians, organizations masked as, i. 115
  Paumanoc, i. 16
Inn, Enoch Story's, ii. 54
Inspirationists, customs and creed of, ii. 200–205
  villages of the, ii. 197–199
Irish channel, ii. 28
Iroquois, League of the, i. 174, 175
  meeting-place of the, i. 205, 212
  mementos of the, i. 189
Irvington, i. 145, 146
Irving, Washington, i. 65
  at Sunnyside, i. 146, 147, 149, 150
  city house of, i. 103, 104
  grave of, i. 147
  rambles of, i. 151, 169; ii. 14

J

Jabey, Brother. See Miller, Peter
Jackson, President, i. 124
James, Richard, Rev., ii. 38, 39
James River, down the, ii. 239–241
Jamestown, ii. 38, 239
  site of, ii. 251, 253
Jamestown Island, ii. 253, 254, 255
Jamestown pioneers, ii. 251
Jay, John, i. 125, 164; ii. 65
Jefferson, Thomas, lodging house of, ii. 67, 73, 259, 270
Jenny Lind, i. 80
Jericho, i. 49–71

282

INDEX

Jersey City, i. 131
Jesuit Fathers, first missionary efforts of, i. 179–181
Job, Andrew, ii. 102
Job, Thomas, ii. 102
Jocelyn, i. 15
Jogues, Father, martyrdom of, i. 179, 180, 182
Johnson family, i. 187
Johnson Hall, i. 185–187, 191
Johnson, John, Sir, i. 177
    driven from Johnson Hall, i. 186, 187
    plans Mohawk invasion, i. 191, 192
Johnson, William, Sir, among the Indians, i. 183
    comes to America, i. 182
    death of, i. 185
    grave of, i. 186
    knighted, i. 184
Johnstown, i. 176, 182
Jumel, Madame, i. 89–92
Jumel mansion, (formerly Morris mansion), i. 85, 140
    present condition of, i. 92, 93, 140
    scenes in, i. 89–91
Jumel, Stephen, i. 89, 90
Junto Club, ii. 56, 57

K

Kaaterskill, i. 212
Kedar, ii. 120
Keens, ii. 44
Kennett Square, ii. 92, 96–98
Kent County, St. Paul's in, ii. 40, 41
Kent Island, ii. 36
    Anglican Church in, ii. 38, 39
    restored to Claiborne, ii. 37
Kent Point, ii. 37

Key, Francis Scott, ii. 30
Kidd, Captain, i. 20, 24, 25
    in the wake of, i. 45, 48
    last voyage of, i. 28, 29
    treasure of, i. 26, 27
Kinderhook, i. 172
King William, i. 61
King's Bridge Road, i. 143, 144
King's College, i. 123
Kingsessing, ii. 46
King's Road, i. 94
Kingston destroyed, i. 167, 168
    head-quarters, i. 223–225
    old Dutch church, i. 219, 220
    Senate House, i. 221, 222
Kiskatom, i. 212
Kitchewan Bay, i. 135
Kitchewan River, i. 135
Klein, George, church built by, ii. 154
    vision of, ii. 153
Knickerbocker literary period, i. 65
Knox, ii. 73
    head-quarters of, ii. 83
Kock, ii. 197
Kosciusko, i. 232
Kossuth, i. 80

L

Lætitia Court, ii. 48
Lætitia House, ii. 47, 48
Lafayette, i. 80, 121, 135
    at Washington's head-quarters, i. 223, 224, 226
    head-quarters of, ii. 83, 145
Lake Agawam, i. 51
Lake Cazenovia, i. 200
Lake Suinipink, i. 234
Lancaster, ii. 92, 107
Lancaster County, ii. 102–104, 153
Landing, the. See Catskill
Lansdowne, ii. 48
Laurens, Colonel, ii. 70

INDEX

Leatherstocking Cave, i. 205
Leatherstocking Falls, i. 205
Lee, Richard Henry, ii. 54, 65
Leeds, i. 209, 211, 214
Lehman, Peter, administration of, ii. 136
    founds Order, ii. 134
Lely, Peter, Sir, ii. 250
Lewis, Anna Estelle (Stella), i. 65
Lewis, Morgan, i. 125, 170
Lexington, battle of, i. 229; ii. 209
Lincoln, Abraham, i. 64
Lind, Jenny, i. 80
Linden Hall, Moravian Female Seminary, ii. 154, 155
Lindenwald, i. 172
Lititz, ii. 149, 152, 155, 158
Little Britain township, ii. 102
Littlefield, Catherine, i. 40
Liverpool and Bristol, trade with, ii. 27
Livingston, Charlotte, i. 125
Livingston, Colonel, i. 153
Livingston, Edward, i. 124
Livingston, Gertrude, i. 125
Livingston, Harriet, i. 130
Livingston, Henry, i. 167, 168
Livingston, Janet, i. 125-128, 169
Livingston, Kate, i. 125, 171
Livingston, Lewis H., i. 171
Livingston manor, i. 122, 129, 131, 159, 234
Livingston mansion, i. 167, 168
Livingston, Peter, i. 123
Livingston, Philip, second lord of the manor, i. 122, 123
Livingston, Philip, signer of the Declaration of Independence, i. 123
Livingston, Robert, first lord of the manor, i. 122, 123

Livingston, Robert R., i. 123
Livingston, Robert R., Chancellor, i. 123,124
    friendship of, i. 129
    mansion built by, i. 132
    sisters of, i. 125
Livingston, Robert R. (second), i. 123, 124
Livingston, Sarah Van Brugh, i. 125
Livingstons, the ablest of all, i. 123
    daughters of, i. 124-127, 132
Livingston, William, i. 123
Lloyd, Edward, ii. 29
Lloyd, Henrietta Maria, ii. 30
Lloyds, the, ii. 30, 32, 33
Locusts, The, i. 169
Logan, Deborah, ii. 52
Logan, Hannah, ii. 52
Logan, James, ii. 49-51
Logan, the Mingo chief, ii. 50
London, i. 129
Long Cove Mountain, i. 153
Longfellow, Henry Wadsworth, i 65
Longfellow's poem, ii. 86
Long Island, i. 13
    battle of, i. 67; ii. 16
    colonial reminders, i. 49, 60
    end of journey in, i. 73
    hills, view of, i. 106
    shore, i. 17, 18, 79
Long Islanders, i. 73
Long Island Sound, i. 41, 43, 45, 68, 103
Longwood Cemetery, ii. 97
Lord Vere, i. 14
Loudon, Lord, i. 159
Louis Philippe, i. 80
    dinner set of, i. 101
Louisiana, cession of, i. 124
    senator from, i. 124

284

INDEX

Love Feast, Moravian, ii. 165–167

Lower Manor, the. See Clermont

Loyalists, i. 144

Ludwick, Baker-General, ii. 71

Lutherans, ii. 108

Lyndhurst, Baron, i. 28

Lynn, men from, i. 49

M

Mack, Alexander, ii. 108

Madison County, i. 200

Madison, James, ii. 53, 73

"Magdalen," man of war, ii. 258

"Manajungh on the Skorkihl," ii. 44

Manchonake, i. 16

Manhattan, i. 143

Manhattan Club, i. 98

Manhattan Island, i. 107

Manheim, ii. 92, 104–106

Manisees. See Block Island

Manors of colonial New York, i. 13

Marble Cemetery, i. 96

Marblehead, ii. 28

Marie Antoinette, furniture of, 190

Marienborn, ii. 109

Marshall, John, encounters Washington, ii. 224–227

Maryland Committee of Safety, ii. 15

Maryland, judges of, ii. 32

Maryland, tariff of, ii. 236

Mary, Queen, ii. 261

Marysville, ii. 158

Mason, ii. 270

Mason, George, ii. 219

Massachusetts, colony of, i. 32

Matteawan Indians, i. 166

Maxwell, Elizabeth, story of, ii. 101, 102

McClellan, ii. 248

McIntosh, widow. See Fillmore, Mrs.

McKean, Thomas, ii. 65

Melrose Abbey, ivy from, i. 149

Mercer, General, i. 88

Mesier homestead, i. 166, 167

Mesier Park, i. 167

Mesier, Peter, i. 166

"Methodist, The," canoe, ii. 24

Metz, Christian, ii. 197

Meyer, Harmanus, journey of, i. 220

Middle Chesapeake, ii. 27

Miles River, ii. 27, 28

Miller, Bernard, ii. 177–179

Miller, Peter, story of, ii. 128–130

Mill Street, ii. 75

Mohawks, i. 175, 211

Mohawks and Tories, horde of, i. 191

Mohawk, the, i. 187, 188, 212

Valley of, i. 174, 179

Mohegan Bluff, i. 30

Mohegans, i. 32

Mohicans, fur trade with, i. 111

Moncock, battle of, ii. 38

Monroe, Elbert, C., i. 155

Mrs., country-place of, i. 154, 155

Monroe, James, last residence of, i. 95, 96

rival of, i. 125

Montauk, gateway of, i. 41

Montauks, i. 17

Montcalm, i. 120, 184

Montgomery County, ii. 79

Montgomery, Fort, i. 233

Montgomery House. See Grassmere

Montgomery, mansion built by, i. 132

Montgomery, Mrs., i. 171

letter of, 128

Montgomery Place, i. 132

Montgomery, Richard, at Rhinebeck, i. 170
marriage of, i. 126, 127
reburial of, i. 128, 129

Montreal, i. 192, 197

Moore House, ii. 269

Moore, William, memorial stone of, ii. 87

Moravian Church, ii. 144
Christmas celebration, ii. 167–172
Easter celebration, ii, 163, 167
faith, converts to, ii. 147–149
Female Seminary, ii. 145
God's Acre, ii. 147
Theological College, ii. 145

Moravians, the, coming of, ii. 139–142
converts to, ii. 147–149
customs of, ii. 146, 147
economy of, ii. 143, 144

Moreau, Marshall, house of, ii. 78

Moriches and Patchogue, land between, i. 61

Morris family, i. 140

Morris, Gouverneur, Chinese gifts of, ii. 221

Morris mansion, i. 86
in Washington's career, i. 87–89

Morris, Mary (Philipse), Mrs., death of, i. 141
marriage of, i. 86, 140
meets Washington, i. 139

Morris, Robert, ii. 26
house of, ii. 71

Morris, Roger, Colonel, i. 86, 89
dies in England, i. 140, 141

Morse, Samuel F. B., city home of, i. 98
triumph of, i. 107, 129

Mount Custis, ii. 19

Mount Independence, i. 232

Mount McGregor, i. 96

Mount Vernon, cares of state at, ii. 222–224
estate of, ii. 219–221
historic rooms, ii. 229–231, 232
mansion of, ii. 218
ownership of, ii. 228, 229
sudden arrivals at, ii. 217
visitors to, ii. 225–227, 234
Washington's early days at, ii. 212–216

Mount Vernon Ladies Association, ii. 229

Mount Vision, i. 204

Mowatt, Anna Cora, i. 65

Muhlenberg, Father, ii. 79–81

Musgrave, Colonel, ii. 69

N

Naples, Bay of, i. 79

Napoleon, i. 122; ii. 78

Narragansetts, i. 17, 32

Nassau Street, i. 82

Nazareth, founding of, ii. 149, 150
present town of, ii. 151

Nazareth Hall, ii. 151, 152

Neck, the, ii. 49

Nelson House, ii. 270

Nelson, Thomas (third), General, ii. 266, 270

Nelson, Thomas (Scotch Tom), ii. 265

Nelson, war horse, ii. 221, 222

Netherlands, Prince of the, i. 111

Neutral ground, the, i. 144

New Amsterdam, i. 49, 77, 78, 148

Newburgh, i. 222
proclamation read at, i. 228, 229
relics at, i. 225, 226

INDEX

New Helvetia, ii. 157
New Jersey, terminus at, i. 107
New Kent, county of, ii. 38
New London, harbor of, i. 36
New Philadelphia Society, ii. 179
Newport Harbor, drowning in, i. 44
New Sweden, ii. 43
New Windsor, i. 229
New York, Bay of, i. 79
　canal, i. 79
　first colonial manor of, i. 13
　first English settlers in, i. 14
　literary reminders of, i. 103–108
　old houses of, i. 82–85
　Presidents who have died in, i. 95
　streets of, i. 77–79, 81
　tracing early days of, i. 76, 77
New York, State of, freedom to slaves in the, i. 70
　vote of, i. 169
Nicholls, Governor, i. 20
Nicoll, Edward, i. 64
Norris, Isaac, home of, ii. 49, 51
Northampton, county of, ii. 10, 15
North Cape, ii. 28
North Carolina and Virginia, boundary of, ii. 246
North, Lord, ii. 261
Nullification Proclamation, the, i. 124

O

O'Conor, Charles, i. 99
Odell, Captain, i. 151, 152
Odell House, i. 151–153
Ohio River, ii. 232
Oldham, Captain John, i. 32

Old Swedes' Church, ii. 44–46
Oneidas, i. 175
Onesimus. See Israel Echerlin, ii. 120
Orange, William of, ii. 53
Order of the Solitary, ii. 119, 128
　decline of, 129
　offspring of, 134
Oriskany, battle of, i. 175, 195–198
Oriskany Falls, i. 176, 192
Orrery, Duke of, ii. 251
Oserneuon, i. 178
Oswego, i. 192
Otis, ii. 263
Otsego Rock, i. 205
Otsego, the, i. 176
Our Lady of Martyrs, Shrine of, i. 182
Oxford, ii. 26, 102
Ox Pasture Road, i. 51
Oyster Bay, i. 49, 68, 69

P

Paca homestead, ii. 33
Paca, Mary (Chew), ii. 32
Paca, William, Governor, ii. 16, 30, 32
　last days of, ii. 35
　picture of, ii. 34
Palace Green, ii. 265
Palatinate of the Rhine, i. 188
Palatine Bridge, i. 176, 187
　named, i. 188, 190
"Palatine," the phantom ship, i. 43, 44
Palisades, i. 88
Palmer, Edward, spy, i. 160, 161
Paoli, massacre at, ii. 90–92
Paris, i. 124
Parker mansion, ii. 11
Parker, name of, ii. 12
Park Row, i. 78
Parton, authority of, i. 91

287

INDEX

Passajungh, ii. 44
Patchogue, i. 49, 64–66
"Patroon's" mansion, i. 116
Patroon system, i. 110, 111
Patroons, the, ii. 110–113
Patterson, Betty, i. 90
Paulding, James Kirk, i. 169
Pawlet family, ii. 244
Pawlet, John, Sir, ii. 244
Payne, John Howard, i. 57
Payne, Mr., contests Washington, ii. 233, 234
Peale, Rembrandt, picture of, ii. 229
Pearl Street, i. 78, 81, 82
Peck Slip, i. 78
Peconic Bay, murder in, i. 52–55
Peekskill, i. 142, 159
Pelletreau House, i. 51
Pemberton country-seat, ii. 49
Pembertons, the three, ii. 51
Pendleton, i. 170
Peniel, ii. 121
"Penn and Logan Correspondence," ii. 52
Penn, descendants of, ii. 55
Penn, John, ii. 48
Penn, Lætitia, ii. 47
Penn, Richard, house of, ii. 71
Pennsbury, ii. 48
Pennsbury Manor, ii. 76–78
Penns, the, ii. 48
Penn's Wood, ii. 76
Pennsylvania, ii. 51
Pennsylvania State Society of the Cincinnati, ii. 88
Penn, William, i. 73; ii. 27, 42
　　founds Philadelphia, ii. 46–48, 50, 57
　　manor-house of, ii. 76–78, 125, 139
Penn, William, second, ii. 54↑
Penn, William, the younger, ii. 54, 55

Pequots, i. 16
Perry, Commodore, bombshells given by, i. 155
Petersborough, Earl of, ii. 250
Petersboro, i. 176, 198
Petersburg, ii. 243
Philadelphia, i. 107; ii. 208
　a last picture of, ii. 72
　city laid out, ii. 46
　City Tavern, ii. 64
　council in, ii. 58
　day's journey from, ii. 92
　first colonial Congress in, ii. 64–68
　girl sold in, ii. 101
　in 1774, ii. 63
　intellectual life of, ii. 56
　old library in, ii. 57
　outings, ii. 75
　polite society of, ii. 52, 53
　State House, ii. 57, 64
　　Declaration signed in, ii. 66–68
　　inauguration in, ii. 72
　Swedes' settlement in, ii. 43–46
　the national capital, ii. 71
Philemon, Lloyd, ii. 29, 32
　daughter of, ii. 32
Philipsburg, house of, i. 138–140
　manor of, i. 110, 132, 137
　warlike scenes in, i. 144
Philipse Castle, i. 138, 146
Philipse family, i. 137, 140
Philipse, Frederick, i. 86
　buildings erected by, i. 137, 138
Philipse, Frederick (third), Colonel, i. 140
　property of, confiscated, i. 141, 154
Philipse, Mary. See Morris, Mary (Philipse), Mrs.
Phillipsburg, Pennsylvania, ii. 179
Pierpont, Samuel, Rev., grave of, i. 46, 47

INDEX

Pierson, Thomas, ii. 92
Platt, Mary, i. 64
Plymouth, ii. 9
Plymouth Rock, i. 32; ii. 36
Pocahontas, ii. 241, 261
Pocantico Creek, i. 138, 146
Poe, Edgar A., i. 65
    at Fordham Cottage, i. 104, 106
Portugal, ii. 28
Posey County, ii. 174
Posey, Major, i. 237
Post Road, beginning of the, i. 159
    New York end of the, i. 143
Potomac, ii. 37
Potomac Company, ii. 236
Potomac Falls, ii. 236
Potts mansion, ii. 85
Poughkeepsie, i. 162, 167, 169
Powder Horn, ii. 257, 260
Presqu' Isle, ii. 88
Prince Edward Island, i. 64
Prince of Orange, i. 15
Prospect Hill. See Genet homestead
Prospect Rock, i. 205
Provincial Assembly, i. 122
Provincials, i. 196
Pulaski's legion, ii. 16
Putnam County, i. 162, 163, 166
Putnam, Fort, i. 232
Putnam, Israel, General, i. 28
    camp of, i. 61, 88
    disposes of a spy, i. 60

Q

Quaker meeting-house, oldest, i. 74; ii. 26
Quakers seek refuge, i. 47; ii. 46, 49, 50, 57
Quebec, expedition against, i. 127, 128, 171, 184

Queen's Head. See Fraunces Tavern
Queen's Rangers, i. 68
Queenstown, ii. 39

R

Radcliffe Street, ii. 75
Raleigh Tavern, ii. 264
Rambos, ii. 44
Ramsay, David, ii. 103
Randolph, Anne, ii. 251
Randolph, Edmund, ii. 263
Randolph, John, ii. 243
    house of, ii. 256
Randolph, Peyton, ii. 65
Randolphs, the, ii. 241 244
    estates of, ii. 243
Rappahannock, anecdote of the, ii. 208
Rapp, George, death of the, ii. 181
    doctrines of, ii. 173
    organizes Harmony Society, ii. 174, 175
    rule of, ii. 176–180
Rapp, Gertrude, ii. 183
Rauch, Christian, missionary, ii. 148, 149
    begins career, ii. 154
Ray, Catherine, i. 40
Red Hook, i. 132
Red Lion Hotel, ii. 264
Reef Tavern, 143
Regents, the, ii. 230
Reidesel, Baron, i. 120
Rensselaer, daughter of the house of, i. 117
Rensselaers, the, ii. 114
Rensselaerwyck, i. 112, 117
Renwick, Mrs., i. 150
Reservoir the, i. 143
Revolutionary era, structures belonging to, i. 77
Revolution, brilliant exploit of the, ii. 16
    church in the, i. 161
    first overt act of the, ii. 257

Revolution, privateering in the, ii. 27, 28
soldier of the, i. 125
Rhinebeck, church at, i. 125, 127, 136
founding of, i. 170, 171
Rhine Palatinates, i. 190
Rhode Island, General Assembly of, i. 33
Richmond, ii. 239, 240
city laid out, ii. 246
Ringgold, Thomas, ii. 16
Ripley, George, i. 65
Rittenhouse, David, observatory built by, ii. 67
River Eder, immersion in the, ii. 108
Rodney, Cæsar, ii. 16, 65
Roe, Edward Payson, i. 230, 231
Rogers, John, first public-house built by, i. 159
Rokeby, i. 132
Rolfe, John, ii. 252
Romans of the New World, i. 174
Rome, i. 191
Roost, the, i. 148
Roslyn, i. 49, 71
Ross, Betsy, Mrs., flag made by, ii. 68, 69
Roxborough, ii. 47
Rudman, ii. 44
Rutledges, the, ii. 65

S

Saal, ii. 133
Sacramento, ii. 158
Sacramento River, ii. 156, 157
Sag Harbor, i. 56, 57
Salem, North Carolina, Easter celebration at, ii. 163–170
Salisbury, Francis, i. 210, 212
Salisbury House, romance of, i. 213, 214

Salisbury, Sylvester, i. 209
Saltonstall, Richard, Sir, i. 28
San Domingo, ii, 255
Sandwich Islands, ii. 156
Sandy Point, i. 42, 43
San Francisco, Bay of, ii. 157
San Juan d'Ulloa, Castle of, i. 155
San Miguel de Guandope, ii. 255
Saratoga, i. 120
Saron, ii. 121, 131–133
Say and Seal, Lord, i. 15
Saybrook, Fort, i. 15, 16, 22
Sayre House, i. 51
Scarborough, i. 145, 155
Scheible, Daniel, ii. 126, 127
Schoharie, settlement of, i. 176–178
Schuckburgh, composer of "Yankee Doodle," i. 117
Schuneman, Johannes, Dominie, i. 210
parsonage of, i. 211
Schute, Sven, Commander, ii. 44
Schuyler, Alida, i. 122
Schuyler, Elizabeth, i. 121
Schuyler family, i. 117
Schuyler House, i. 117, 118
panorama from, i. 120
visitors to, i. 121
Schuyler, Johannes, Dominie, i. 176
Bible used by, i. 177
Schuyler manor-house, i. 117, 118
panorama from, i. 120
Schuyler, Peter, i. 117, 121
Schuyler, Philip, General, i. 94, 117
attempted capture of, i. 118, 119
entertains Burgoyne, i. 120, 121
Schuylers, the, i. 132
Schuyler Street, i. 117

INDEX

Schuylerville, i. 121
  mansion at, i. 117
Schuylkill, ii. 43, 59
Schuylkill Valley, ii. 90
Scott, General, i. 155
  old home of, i. 97
Second Maryland Regiment,
  ii. 16
Second Street, ii. 48
Separatists, celibacy of the,
  ii. 194–196
  settlement of the, ii. 108,
  189, 193
Settlers, first English, i. 14
Seventh Street, ii. 49
Severn, the, ii. 28
Seward, William A., i. 114
Shaefferstown, ii. 105
Shekomo, mission of, ii. 149
Shelter Island, i. 22, 45, 49
  name of, i. 48
  occupation of, i. 47
Sherman, Roger, ii. 65
Shewell, Elizabeth, ii. 94–96
Shinnecock Hills, i. 52
Shinnecock Indians, i. 52, 53
Shinnecock Neck, i. 52
Shirley, ii. 239
  manor-house of, ii. 241–243
Shoharius, i. 154
Sigourney, Lydia, Mrs., i. 65
Simancas, ii. 254
Simcoe, Colonel, i. 68
Sinclair, Catherine, i. 99
Sing Sing, i. 155, 156
Sisters' House, ii. 145
Sitka, ii. 156
Six Nations, i. 174
  land of the, i. 174, 176,
  178, 187, 201, 206
Skinners, i. 136, 144, 148
Sleepy Hollow, church at, i.
  146, 147
Smallwood's regiment ii.
  15, 16
Smiley, Samuel, ii. 89
Smith, Eliza Oakes, i. 65,
  66
Smith, Gerrit, i. 198

Smith, John, Captain, ii. 252,
  254
Smith, John, marriages of, i.
  63, 64
Smith, Seba, i. 64, 65
Smith, Tangier. See Smith,
  Colonel William
Smith, Tangier, family, i.
  62
Smith, William, born 1777,
  i. 64
Smith, William, Colonel, i.
  61
Smith, William, Judge, i. 63
Snow Hill, ii. 22
  monastical Society of, ii.
  134–138
  nunnery of, ii. 134
Society of Friends, ii. 98,
  100
Southampton, i. 56
  modern prosperity of, i. 51
  whale-fishery of, i. 50
Southeastern Pennsylvania,
  hamlets of, ii. 92
South Street, i. 81
Southwark, ii. 43, 45, 49
Spangenburg, Bishop, ii.
  151
Southwell, Robert, Sir, ii.
  251
Spotswood, Alexander, Sir,
  ii. 257
  house of, ii. 269
Spuyten Duyvil Creek, i.
  137, 143
Stage route, old, i. 142, 143
Stanton, i. 125
State of New York, first con-
  stitution of, i. 124
States-General, i. 112
State Street, No. 7, i. 79, 81
"St. David's at Radnor,
  Old," ii. 86–89
Stenton, ii. 49
  social life at, ii. 50–52
Sterling, Earl of, i. 19
Steuben, Baron, i. 135 ; ii. 211
  grave of, i. 198, 199

INDEX

Stewart, Alexander T., old house of, i. 97
St. George's Church, i. 75
St. George's Manor, i. 49, 60–64
Stiegel, Baron, ii. 92
   reception of, ii. 104
   rent paid to, ii. 105
Stillwater, i. 212
Stirling, Lord, ii. 16
St. James Church, ii. 154
St. John's church-yard, i. 186
St. Leger, Colonel, i. 194
St. Luke's Protestant Episcopal Church, i. 93
St. Mary's, ii. 37
St. Michael's, vessels of, ii. 27, 28, 30
Stone Street, i. 78
Stony Point, i. 157
   capture of, i. 235–237
Strand, the. See Catskill
Stuyvesant, Governor, i. 147
Sun Inn, the, ii. 145
Sunnyside, cottage of, i. 146
   history of, i. 147, 148
   life in, i. 150
   restoration of, i. 149
Susquehanna, i. 204, 205 ; ii. 103
   depicted by Cooper, i. 206
Sutter, John A., General, claim of, ii. 158
   discovers gold, ii. 157
   grave of, ii. 155, 156, 159
Swanson, ii. 44
Swanson, Swan, ii. 46
Swarthmore, ii. 92–94, 96
Swedes, ii. 47
Swift, Joseph, ii. 103
Swiss Guard, ii. 156
Sylvester, Brinley, of Newport, i. 48
Sylvester, Grissell Brinley, i. 47, 48
   Mrs., i. 47, 48
Sylvester Island. See Shelter Island

Sylvester Manor, i. 48, 49
Sylvester, Nathaniel, i. 47
   Quaker guests of, i. 47, 48
Sylvester, Nathaniel and Grissell, lineal descendants of, i. 48

T

Tabea, Sister, story of, ii. 125–128
Talleyrand, i. 80, 200
Tangier Island, ii. 24, 25
Tangier Sound, ii. 22, 23
Tappan Sea, Flying Dutchman of the, i. 150, 151
Tappan, village of, i. 153, 237, 238
Tarrytown, i. 138, 145, 153–155
Taylor, Bayard, ii. 96–98
Taylor, Mary Agnew, ii. 97
Tekagwita, Catherine, i. 179, 181, 182
Teller's Point, i. 153
Third Street, ii. 49
Thomas Boyle, Captain, ii. 28
Thome, Margaret. See Sister Tabea
Thomson, Charles, ii. 67, 223
Threadhaven Creek, ii. 26
Tilghman, Edward, ii. 16
Tilghman, Matthew Ward, ii. 15
Tilghman, Richard, ii. 40
Tilghman, Tench, Lieutenant-Colonel, ii. 16
Tivoli, i. 131, 132
Tolstoi, Leo, Count, ii. 173
Tories, Johnson's, i. 196
   prison for, i. 168, 169
   under arms, ii. 15
Town Pond. See Lake Agawan
Townsend, Captain, i. 65
Townsend homestead, i. 68, 69

INDEX

Trappe, church at, ii. 79–81
Trenton, i. 131
Tribes, Long Island, i. 18
Trinity church-yard, i. 131
Tryon General, attempt of, i. 135, 161
  rendezvous of, i. 66
Tryon County, militia of, i. 192
Tschoop, conversion of, ii. 147–149
Turnbull, Jim, i. 54–56
Turner, Edith, i. 55–56
Turner Joseph, ii. 49
Tweed, William M., dwellings of, i. 98
Tyler, President, i. 28

U

Ulster County, founders of, i. 209
United Netherlands Company, i. 111
United States Supreme Court, ii. 158
Upper Brandon, ii. 248
Upper Hudson, i. 160
Utica, i. 176, 193

V

Valley Creek, ii. 82, 83
Valley Forge, i. 198
  camp at, ii. 63, 79
  site of, ii. 81–83
  Washington's headquarters at, ii. 82, 85
Van Bergen, Marten, i. 209, 210
Van Buren, Martin, i. 172
Van Cortlandt, James Stevenson, i. 136
Van Cortlandt, John, i. 134
Van Cortlandt manor, i. 132–136
  manor-house, i. 157
Van Cortlandt, Pierre, i. 135
Van Cortlandts, descent of the, i. 134

Van Cortlandt, Stephanus, i. 133, 157
Vancouver, ii. 156
Van Dam, Rambout, i. 151
Vanderbilt, Commodore, house of, i. 97
Vanderlyn, John, i. 217–219
Van Rensselaer, Johannes, i. 112
Van Rensselaer, Killian, i. 112, 132
Van Rensselaer, Stephen, General, i. 112
  leases farms, i. 113
Van Rensselaer, Stephen, sixth of the line, i. 112, 113
  wife of, i. 119
Van Rensselaer, William, i. 113
Van Rensselaers, the, i. 115, 116, 132
Van Tassel, Jacob, i. 148
  wife of, i. 148
Van Tassel, Laney, i. 148
Van Vost, family of, i. 186
Van Wart, i. 154
Varina, ii. 241
Varnum, General, ii. 84
Vaughan, General, i. 235
Vera Cruz, i. 155
Vernon, Admiral, ii. 211
Verplanck's Point, i. 158, 235
Verrazani, i. 32
Versailles, ii. 156
Viking boat, i. 36, 37
Virginia, capital of, ii. 256, 267–269
  State of, request of the, i. 96
Von Linklaen, Jan, i. 200
"Vulture," the, i. 153

W

Waerden, i. 14
Wales, Prince of, ii. 240
Wallace, James, Sir, i. 167

INDEX

Wallace, John, story of, i. 58–60

Wallack, Lester and James W., early homes of, i. 99

Wall Street, i. 76, 78

Waln, Nicholas, ii. 51

Walpole, Robert, Sir, ii. 251

Wappinger's Falls, i. 162, 166

Wappingi Indians, i. 166

Ward, Matthew, ii. 16

Warner, Anna, i. 232

Warner, Susan, i. 231, 232

War of 1812, ii. 16

"Warrior," wreck of the, i. 42

Warwick, ii. 153

Warwick Furnace, ii. 90

Washington, Augustine (first), ii. 207, 208
(second), ii. 207

Washington, Bushrod, ii. 228

Washington, George, i. 49, 67, 86, 121, 126, 173, 184, 226 ; ii. 16, 53
adventure of, i. 87–89
appearance of, ii. 215
appoints a baker, ii. 71
as commander-in-chief, ii. 216, 217
at Valley Forge, ii. 82, 84, 85, 90, 145
soldiers of, ii. 155
at West Point, i. 235
council chamber, i. 92
crosses the Delaware, ii. 79
designs flag, ii. 68, 69
dies at Mount Vernon, ii. 228
encounter with Payne, ii. 233, 234
head-quarters of, i. 87
house occupied by, i. 75
in Alexandria, ii. 232, 235–237, 267
inauguration of, i. 124
in Congress, ii. 65, 66
in the South, i. 120

Washington, George, last public appearance of, ii. 73, 74
last vote of, ii. 238, 270
lays foundations of capital, ii. 223
love-affairs of, ii. 213
manages estate, ii. 219–221
marriage of, ii. 214
persuades Marshall to enter Congress, ii. 224, 227
Philadelphia dwelling of, ii. 72
physician of, i. 170
questions Wayne, i. 235, 236
reply of Gates, i. 227, 228
returns to Mount Vernon, ii. 218, 224
returns to New York, i. 84
summoned to resume his arms, ii. 228
takes farewell in Fraunces's tavern, i. 83
takes possession of Mount Vernon, ii. 212
with his mother, ii. 206–211

Washington Heights, i. 86, 140

Washington, Jane, Mrs., ii. 228

Washington, John Augustine, ii. 228
(second), ii. 228

Washington, Lawrence, ii. 207, 211–213

Washington, Martha, Mrs., i. 40, 223–226 ; ii. 12, 13, 53
as Martha Custis, ii. 214, 215
brave words of, ii. 216
dies, ii. 228

INDEX

Washington, Martha, Mrs., joins her husband, ii. 217, 218
marries General Washington, ii. 214
Washington, Mary (Ball), Mrs., ii. 207-211
Washington's army, i. 136
Water Serpent, story told by the, i. 54-56
Water Street, i. 81
Watson, ii. 49
Wayne, Anthony, General, i. 235-237
at Paoli, ii. 90, 91
grave of, ii. 88
homestead of, ii. 89
Wayne, Isaac, Colonel, ii. 88
Waynesboro, ii. 134
Webb, James Watson, i. 154
present to, i. 155
Webber, Wolfert, i. 78
Weehauken, i. 94
Weems, Parson, ii. 207, 208
Welcome Creek, ii. 76
Wells family, i. 187
West, Benjamin, i. 129; ii. 92
paints first picture, ii. 93
romance of, ii. 94, 95
Westchester County, i. 160, 163
Westchester, passage from the history of, i. 109
Western Maryland, ii. 37
Western Shore, ii. 37
West Indies, ii. 27, 28, 53
West, John, ii. 93
Westmoreland, ii. 207
Westover, ii. 55, 239, 248
magnificence of, ii. 246, 247
patent of, ii. 244
Westover House, ii. 244-247
West Point, i. 229, 231, 232
West Walnut Lane, hospital at, ii. 70
Wharton House, ii. 49
Wharton, Robert, Mayor, ii. 88

Whigs, houses of, fired at, i. 167
Whitefield, i. 136
buys land, ii. 150
in Pennsylvania, ii. 150
Whitemarsh Church, ii. 26
White Plains, i. 164
Whitesboro, i. 193
Whitsuntide, ii. 18
Wickhams, the, ii. 241
"Widgeon," the steamer, ii. 19
Widman, Michael, spy, ii. 128-130
Widow's House, ii. 147
William and Mary College, ii. 256, 262, 263
Williamsburg, ii. 239, 255, 256, 260-264
Williams, David, i. 154
grave of, i. 178
Wildercroft, i. 132
Willemson, Mary, wife of Lion Gardiner, i. 14
Willis, Nathaniel P., i. 65, 99
closing years of, i. 229, 230
Wilson, Alexander, ii. 46, 60
Wilson, Marinus, Colonel, i. 191
Wilton, ii. 49
Wiltwyck burying-ground, i. 217, 219
Winthrop, John, i. 15, 45
the younger, i. 45
Winthrop, Theodore, ii. 261
Winthrop, Wait Still, i. 46
Winthrops, the, of Fisher's Island, i. 45, 47
manor house of, i. 46
Wistar House, ii. 70
Wittgenstein, ii. 107
Wolfe, i. 184
Woodlands, ii. 49
World's Fair, i. 36
Wren, Christopher, Sir, ii. 260
Wright, Silas, i. 115

295

INDEX

Wyandance, chief of the Montauks, i. 17
Wye House, ii. 28–30
  first master of, ii. 29, 32
  grandeur of, ii. 33, 35
  visit of Frederick Douglas to, ii. 31, 32
Wye Island, ii. 18, 33, 35
Wye River, ii. 29, 30, 36

Y

Yonkers, city hall of, i. 138, 145
York, Duke of, i. 78, 238
York River, ii. 265

Yorktown, ii. 209, 239
  a trading centre, ii. 260, 265
  struggle in, ii. 267, 269, 270
Young, John, i. 115
Young, Mr., i. 164

Z

Zinzendorf, Count, Moravian leader, ii. 139–141, 150, 151
  christens Lititz, ii. 155
  visits Warwick, ii. 153
Zion, ii. 121

THE END